The Great Generals Series

This distinguished new series features the lives of eminent military leaders who changed history in the United States and abroad. Top military historians write concise but comprehensive biographies including the personal lives, battles, strategies, and legacies of these great generals, with the aim to provide background and insight into today's armies and wars. These books are of interest to the military history buff, and, thanks to fast-paced narratives and references to current affairs, they are also accessible to the general reader.

Patton by Alan Axelrod

Grant by John Mosier

Eisenhower by John Wukovits

LeMay by Barrett Tillman

MacArthur by Richard B. Frank

Stonewall Jackson by Donald A. Davis

Bradley by Alan Axelrod

Pershing by Jim Lacey

Andrew Jackson by Robert V. Remini

Sherman by Steven E. Woodworth

Lee by Noah Andre Trudeau

Marshall by H. Paul Jeffers

Pershing

Jim Lacey

palgrave
macmillan

First published in hardcover in 2008 by PALGRAVE
MACMILLAN® in the US—a division of St. Martin's Press
LLC, 175 Fifth Avenue, New York, NY 10010.

Where this book is distributed in the UK, Europe and the rest of
the world, this is by Palgrave Macmillan, a division of Macmillan
Publishers Limited, registered in England, company number
785998, of Houndmills, Basingstoke, Hampshire RG21 6XS.

Palgrave Macmillan is the global academic imprint of the above
companies and has companies and representatives throughout the
world.

Palgrave® and Macmillan® are registered trademarks in the
United States, the United Kingdom, Europe and other countries.

ISBN: 978-0-230-61445-1

Library of Congress Cataloging-in-Publication Data
Lacey, Jim, 1958–
    Pershing / James Lacey.
        p.   cm.
    ISBN 0-230-60383-1 (alk. paper)
    1. Pershing, John J. (John Joseph), 1860–1948.
2. Generals—United States—Biography.   3. United States
Army—Biography.   4. United States. Army—History—
Punitive Expedition into Mexico, 1916.   5. World War,
1914–1918—United States.   I. Title.
E181.P478   2008
355.0092—dc22
[B]

                                        2007041691

A catalogue record of the book is available from the British
Library.
First PALGRAVE MACMILLAN paperback edition: June 2009
10 9 8 7 6 5 4 3 2 1
Printed in the United States of America.

Contents

Photosection appears between pages 98 and 99

Foreword

GENERAL OF THE ARMIES—FIVE-STAR GENERAL—JOHN J.
Pershing was America's greatest military leader of the twentieth
century. Pragmatic, duty-driven, fearless, fit, and demanding, he
was a soldier's soldier, America's first and greatest expeditionary
commander, and the architect of the spirit and backbone of America's armies that fought not only World War I, but also World War
II, Korea, and Vietnam. His command style persists to this day as
the *beau ideal* of American leadership.

Yet how can it be that his name doesn't ring off the lips of
commentators and historians, and why isn't he commonly acknowledged along with Eisenhower, MacArthur, or Marshall? Jim
Lacey's incisive biography of Pershing explains this oversight.

From a middle class Midwestern family, John Pershing was industrious and capable, if not a brilliant student. His strength was
his particular intensity of character, his convictions, and sense of
purpose. Entering West Point as one of the oldest in his class, his
bearing, demeanor, and competence earned him the coveted position of First Captain, the top-ranking cadet.

He proved his mettle immediately following graduation, earning respect and admiration from his troops in his first assignment as a lieutenant on the Western frontier in the last of the Indian campaigns. As a captain he wrangled an assignment that brought him to combat in Cuba during the Spanish-American War, and later he became one of the most effective mid-level commanders in the Philippines campaign in the early 1900s.

In every case, Pershing's pragmatism shone through. He wasn't a commander given to needless violence or doctrinaire solutions, but rather judged his team and opponents carefully, chose his fights with care, and then fought with fierce passion to win. In the Philippines he became adept at combining his tactical skills with the kind of low-level diplomacy that isolates adversaries and builds allies. He used force reluctantly, but with extraordinary efficiency. Our Army in Iraq—a century later—seems to have rediscovered Pershing's approach only after three years of tactical stumbles.

The tragic loss of his young wife and three daughters to a house fire in 1915 shattered Pershing's mid-life, but may have further honed his single-minded dedication to duty. In the aftermath of this personal tragedy, during his leadership of the Mexican expedition against Pancho Villa and later in the expedition to France, his intensity and focus literally drove the army.

John Pershing was a hard man. And in the strife and turbulence of alliance warfare he became even more determined and single-minded. In 1917, as the Great War surged into its fourth summer of slaughter, he arrived in France as the designated commander of a not-yet-built American expeditionary force. The British and French armies were exhausted—all they wanted was America's manpower—not America's leadership. It was Pershing, and Pershing alone who stood for an independent American force, who saw the need, organized the staffs, selected the commanders, and built an Army which eventually numbered two million soldiers, fought, and won the decisive final battles of World War I. No one but Pershing could have done it.

Alliance warfare is a snake-pit. I know, as some eighty years later I was in Pershing's position as the senior American commander in Europe. National vanities, huge egos, conflicting military and political ambitions, fear, and pride swirl in a crazy spin of orders, plans, technology, doctrine, and guidance. Pershing was the first American to experience this, and he succeeded brilliantly. His example paved the way for Eisenhower, Marshall, MacArthur, Ridgway, and even Westmoreland, and Abrams. And in my Belgian headquarters, during the 1999 Kosovo crisis, I often looked up at the portrait of General of the Army Pershing that I had borrowed from our embassy in Paris, and sought inspiration. He fended off the overweening allied commanders and their heads of state, wrestled with military rivals in Washington, and worked magic in building and leading a fighting Army that represented America well and was decisive in winning the First World War.

If he had a fault, it was in underestimating the training needs of the American units. The Germans had implemented a new style of tactics, enabled by modern weaponry, to break the stalemate of trench warfare. Called Hutier tactics, the strategy consisted of small cohesive, highly lethal teams which could infiltrate, bypass resistance, and strike deep inside enemy positions in order to avoid frontal assault and destroy the cohesion of prepared defenses.

Used in Eastern Europe, then against the Italians at Caporetto in 1917, and then against the French and British in early 1918, these tactics achieved remarkably better results than simply moving a mass of men frontally against the trench lines. But it required extensive small unit training and discipline.

Pershing, on the other hand, favored spirit, ardor, resolve, and toughness. In essence he had imbibed too much of the French and British rhetoric—and it was also a natural manifestation of his character—without sufficiently understanding the tactical dynamics of a battlefield saturated with machine guns, cannons, poison gas, and aircraft. Pershing tended to work the American Army from the top down, working to establish structure, headquarters, commanders, and a whole logistics and procurement system. It was a monumental effort of heroic proportions, and it built a two million-man force within a few months. On the other hand, the Germans, with a three-year head start, had learned to work the problem of the trench-line stalemate from the bottom up. The battle was imbalanced. The result was incredibly high American casualties during the major and last American campaign, the Meuse-Argonne, in September and October, 1918. And though superior American strength eventually won out, the cost of victory was frightful in terms of casualties.

As for Pershing, he maintained a distance as a commander. In the three short and bloody months of the final campaign, he was the driving force behind both the victory and the slaughter, demanding uncompromising aggressiveness that simply consumed American units. Unlike another American general, Grant, who fought the same way, he wasn't loved. Perhaps it was his distance from the battlefield. Perhaps it was the briefness of the final campaign. Perhaps it was the absence of prior American failures. Perhaps it was the expeditionary nature of the fight (he saved France, not America.) Or maybe it was that he didn't have an Army "sponsor" in Washington, but instead had rivals.

He still emerged from the war with an incredible reputation, but at home it quickly dissolved with the return to American isolationism and pacifism.

Nevertheless, Pershing left an indelible stamp on the Army. He picked and groomed future leaders—MacArthur, Marshall, even Eisenhower. He set up a school system to embed his organizational blueprint that carried the Army through Vietnam and still persists today. And his emphasis on spirit, drive, and open warfare animated the U.S. Army in every campaign through the Gulf War. It wasn't until the 1990s that we really fixed the training problem inside Army units, and addressed the issue of "bottom-up" warfare that has been identified as one of Pershing's main failures as a general.

—*General Wesley K. Clark*

Introduction

THE CRISIS CAME TOWARD THE END OF OCTOBER 1918, IN a forested area most Americans had never heard of, the Meuse-Argonne. For almost a month, over a million American soldiers pounded their way forward against forty German divisions, defending positions so impenetrable that American soldiers wondered if the devil himself had designed them. Already, 100,000 Americans had fallen and General "Black Jack" Pershing's assault divisions were on their last legs. The German line showed no sign of cracking, and there was widespread speculation that the American army might be the first to break.

With the blood of 100,000 Americans staining French soil and only paltry gains, Allied generals and politicians stepped up their verbal barrage on the inadequacies of the American army and General Pershing in particular. On the eve of the Meuse-Argonne offensive, the supreme commander of the Allied effort, Field Marshal Ferdinand Foch, tried to divide the American army among the Allies. When Pershing stymied that attempt, Foch next tried inserting a French army in the middle of the American battle line, to dilute Pershing's operational control. Failing that, Foch then attempted to place a French general in every American division to act as an "advisor."

Foch and Pershing had almost come to blows when Foch ordered that the American army be distributed all along the Allied front. During that encounter, Pershing tried to make the field marshal see reason, but when Foch still insisted on fragmenting the American army, Pershing replied, "Marshal Foch you may insist all you please, but I decline absolutely to agree to your plan. While our army will fight wherever you may decide, it will not fight except as an independent American Army!" Unable to eviscerate the American army, Foch was now trying the next best thing. He would remove that army's leader.

Official French and British diplomatic delegations visited President Woodrow Wilson to inform him that Pershing was not up to the task and requested his removal. With the exception of General Philippe Petain, every major Allied politician, diplomat, and general joined the chorus. By October 1918, they had just one chant: "Pershing must go." On October 9, General Foch, almost certainly acting on the orders of French Premier Georges Clemenceau, issued orders relieving Pershing of command of the American First Army and assigning him to a quiet sector of the front. As Foch had no authority to relieve another Allied commander, this was an incredibly foolish act, and why he thought the Americans would stand for it has never received an explanation.

Foch, however, was not prepared to walk into the lion's den himself, so he sent his deputy, General Maxime Weygand, to deliver the order. The conversation between Pershing and Weygand is not recorded, but one of Pershing's aides, hearing his boss shouting in a titanic rage, turned to Weygand's aide and apologized for the "unimaginable horrors" Weygand was being subjected to. Eventually, Pershing's tirade relented, and Weygand beat a hasty retreat from Pershing's presence, only pausing long enough to call Foch and tell him, "It's all off."

When presented with an opportunity to criticize Pershing, Allied generals displayed a unique ability to forget the fact that they had already led over ten million of his men to slaughter. The truth is that Allied leaders were not really concerned with Pershing's generalship. In fact, he was doing too good of a job for their liking. What they really wanted was for Pershing, his staff, and his senior commanders to embarrass themselves so that these Allied leaders could press their case for disbanding the American army in order to fill their own depleted ranks. Knowing this, neither President Wilson's nor Secretary of War Newton Baker's confidence in Pershing ever waned, and theirs were the only two opinions that mattered. It helped that Baker was in France at the time and making his own assessment of the army and its commander. What he saw impressed him.

In the span of two weeks, Pershing and his First American Army had wiped out the supposedly impregnable salient at St. Mihiel and then, even as that fight was still raging, redeployed over a million men to an entirely different sector and launched it into one of the largest assaults of the war. As in any great endeavor, Pershing's Meuse-Argonne offensive was hampered by a certain degree of confusion and chaos. The First Army was a new formation and many of its troops were experiencing their first taste of combat. Moreover, they were also facing almost forty of the best combat divisions in the German army, defending positions they had been improving for over four years. It was an almost impossible task. Not surprisingly, progress was slow.

Under pressure to show progress that would justify the toll, Pershing pushed his officers and men relentlessly. From dawn until long after dark, he was out visiting the army's forward combat units and through sheer force of his own will inching them forward. Still, the Germans showed no sign of cracking, and American losses were running at almost 5,000 a day.

This was a pattern with which every Allied senior general was familiar. They would launch offensives that would make small gains until the Germans reinforced the sector. From that point on, they would just throw hordes of humans at the German positions until their units had bled out and could no longer endure the carnage. This is what every Allied general expected of Pershing and no one had reason to believe he would act any differently. But Pershing had one asset that is distinctive of all great combat commanders: the ability to learn from mistakes. Seeing that what he was doing was not working, Pershing ceased all attacks in the Meuse-Argonne and stood the entire American army down for almost ten days, not just to reorganize, but also to retrain.

Ignoring repeated pleas from Allied generals, politicians, and diplomats to resume the attack, Pershing put the First Army through an intensive training regimen based on the lessons they had learned in the previous weeks of fighting. As the combat formations remade themselves, Pershing strained to get roads reconditioned, railroads built, and hundreds of thousands of tons of supplies moved forward despite grueling conditions. When the army and its logistical base were ready, Pershing ordered his men forward.

The army that advanced this time was qualitatively superior to the one that had been fighting just two weeks before. It was rested, fed, and confident. Just as important, it had learned: to coordinate the infantry advance with artillery support, to use air support properly, and most of all, it now knew how to first maneuver around strong-points and then to methodically reduce them with minimal losses. In just hours, the remade American First Army broke through the German line. By the end of the second day of the attack it was moving so fast it was running off the maps posted at Pershing's headquarters.

Slightly over a week later, on the eleventh hour of the eleventh day of the eleventh month, World War I ended. Although the Allies, for political reasons, did all they could to minimize the American contribution, German generals without hesitation stated the "war was lost in the Argonne." Without Pershing's assaults chewing up over three dozen German divisions and opening the door to the German heartland, victory could not have been achieved.

The Meuse-Argonne campaign was Pershing's defining moment. He had withstood the political and diplomatic pressure, and endured the heart-sickening casualty reports, while remaining unalterably fixed on his objective. It was the culminating moment of the relentless effort and single-minded determination Pershing demonstrated as he built a two-million-man American army from virtually nothing.

If there were ever a time or an achievement where one man should receive credit for the accomplishments of many thousands, this was it. Without Pershing there would have been no American army to help win World War I. Similarly, if the army he built had been deprived of his drive and command genius at any time during the Battle of Meuse-Argonne, it is almost impossible to believe it would have achieved its spectacular victory.

CHAPTER 1

Born in War

AT 4:00 P.M. ON JUNE 18, 1863, THIRTY SOUTHERN RAIDERS commanded by Clifton Holtzclaw stormed into Laclede, Missouri, shot up and then sacked the town. The Civil War was in its third year and Missouri was suffering under a scourge of raiders who swarmed about the contested border state like locusts, leaving death and wreckage in their wake. Pershing's father, also named John, was in his store, which fronted on the town square, as the raiders rode in. Since his young son, only three at the time, accompanied him to work, the store shotgun was kept unloaded. There was no time to load it, so John Pershing Sr. just turned and locked the safe, which also stored many of the townsfolk's valuables, picked up his shotgun, and strode out the back door with his young son under his arm.

The Pershings lived only five doors down from the store and John Sr. stole in the back door of his home just as two raiders were leaving from the front, convinced by Mrs. Pershing that her husband was not there. He loaded the gun, then walked to the window, raised the gun, and took aim in the direction of his store. Mrs. Pershing, instantly grasping the situation, threw her arms around her husband and begged him not to do anything rash. As the raiders were robbing his store, she pleaded, "You'll be killed. Let the money go." Pershing came to his senses and lowered his rifle. Eventually, a train full of Union soldiers approached the town and the raiders decamped. They took with them property worth about $3,000 and left several dead Laclede citizens in their wake.

Thus, at the tender age of three, John Joseph Pershing, future commander of all American forces in Europe during World War I, chief of staff of the army and General of the Armies of the United States, had his first taste of war. All he later remembered of the incident was that he was scared his father would be killed and that his mother had almost crushed him, as she kept him pinned to the floor with her foot throughout the ordeal.

When John Joseph Pershing was born on September 13, 1860, the country was on the eve of civil war. Though Pershing's only memory of the war was the faded images of this terrifying encounter, it still had a profound influence on his life. Throughout his youth he thrilled at the stories of returning veterans, and though they did not inspire him to pursue a military career, they were deeply embedded his memory.

During his early life, Pershing's family was not rich, but they were comfortably well off. As Pershing remembered it:

> [It] was a time of prosperity and father and mother had hopes of sending all us children eventually to college. Farming was profitable and business at the store was flourishing. One day I overheard a clerk say that father was regarded as one of the wealthiest men in the county. For a time I could picture myself as a student at a college and then at law school. Apparently there was not a cloud

in the business sky. Money was plentiful, prices of commodities were increasing; wages were good; and people were spending freely and incurring new financial obligations without hesitation.[1]

Pershing's father was aggressively incurring debts and had invested his entire worth, plus borrowed funds, in land speculation. This idyllic start came to a crashing end in the Panic of 1873, arguably the worst financial shock the United States has ever suffered, with the exception of the Great Depression. When it struck, Pershing was too young to understand what was happening until one day his father took him aside and explained the extent of the family's troubles. Pershing was abruptly brought face to face with the realities of life, and the revelation that his father was close to bankruptcy made a deep impression on him. At the same time, he felt proud, as for the first time he was being trusted with the responsibilities of manhood.

The store was shuttered and the bank foreclosed on most of Pershing's land holdings. To make ends meet, John Sr. hit the road as a traveling salesman, while thirteen-year-old John Jr. and his younger brother quit school to become full-time farmers. Luck, however, continued to be against young Pershing. In young Pershing's first year as a farmer he was beset by drought and the next year a plague of locusts destroyed his crop. It was hard, but Pershing counted his family luckier than many other local families and he later wrote, "There was no depression in the morale of the family." It was a difficult three years before the family's prospects minimally revived, but Pershing found the experience worthwhile nonetheless because "as difficult as times were, I learned more of the practical side of life than during any similar period."

Young John eventually returned to school. Despite often missing classes due to his duties on the farm, Pershing kept up with his school work during the evening. By the age of eighteen he had passed the test to be a teacher. He applied at a local school about ten miles from Laclede and, despite his youth, the board decided to give him a chance. Previous teachers had left because they could not maintain discipline among the older children, several of whom were older and larger than Pershing. In his second week, the boys, who had forced out his predecessor, decided it was time to test Pershing. After acting up in class, Pershing told them to stay after the rest of the class was dismissed. When they defied him and got up to walk out, Pershing slowly approached the largest of the boys, and calmly informed him, "I am here to run this school and you will obey my orders. If you do not take your seat I will thrash you on this spot." Seeing that Pershing was deadly earnest, the troublemaker took his seat and that was the end of discipline problems. Pershing called his early teaching experience the best lessons he ever had in the art of managing others.

Pershing used the money he earned teaching to attend a small local college at Kirksville, and dreamed of getting enough education to become a lawyer. It was at one of his intermittent stays at Kirksville that he spotted a newspaper notice for a competitive examination for West Point. The test was two weeks away and Pershing took leave from his courses to prepare himself. At the time, he had no thought of a military career and merely saw West Point as a free education and an opportunity to eventually go to law school. When Pershing arrived for the test he found himself pitted against thirteen other applicants for one slot. That number was narrowed down to two after the written test, and Pershing was one of them. The final selection came down to a single question on the oral exam: parse the sentence "I love to run." His competitor said "to run" was an adverbial clause, while Pershing said it was the object of the verb. On this minor grammatical point rested Pershing's fate and by extension, America's. Pershing was right and won the appointment.

+>==<+

Pershing arrived at West Point in 1882, at 5'9" and a muscular 155 pounds. He claimed to be twenty-two years old, which was probably a lie, just under the age limit for a new cadet. Knowing that there was one more test to take before entrance into the academy, Pershing arrived four months early to be tutored along with several other perspective cadets by a former Confederate officer with a reputation for getting his charges past this final barrier to entry. It was also during this time that Pershing got his first glimpse of General Ulysses S. Grant and long afterward he would tell how thrilled he was by the experience. A little over three years later, Pershing, now Cadet Captain, marched the entire corps of cadets several miles from West Point to present themselves along the rail line when Grant's funeral train passed. Until his death, Pershing considered Grant the greatest general the United States had ever produced.

Pershing was one of 104 (out of 144) who passed the final test and was admitted into the West Point Class of 1886. Although a middling student, through dogged persistence he graduated thirtieth out of the seventy-seven cadets who made it through all four years. He was particularly plagued by French and never achieved any practical ability in the language. If not the best student in the class, he was definitely the class leader in every other regard. Robert Bullard, who was a year ahead of Pershing and would later command the Second Army in the American Expeditionary Force (AEF), said of him, "His exercise of authority, was then and always has been since, of a nature peculiarly impersonal, dispassionate, hard, and firm. This quality did not in him, as in many, give offense; the man was too impersonal, too given over to pure business and duty. His manner carried to the minds of those under him the suggestion, nay, the conviction, of unquestioned right to obedience."[2]

But Pershing was not all business. He was known as a "hop man." He never missed an opportunity to attend one of the many dances at West Point or other local social events. Even as a cadet he was known for, in the delicate phrasing of the period, "enjoying the society of women." It was a characteristic of his nature that was to last a lifetime. Even during World War I his staff would go out of its way to make sure there were women at headquarters for Pershing to socialize with at dinner, as it always seemed to improve the boss's mood. Pershing was also selected class president, a position he held until his death, and was selected to the highest cadet rank each year until finally becoming first captain of the Cadet Corps. Later he said that no rank he ever attained after that gave him as much satisfaction.

While at the academy, Pershing had the opportunity to observe the character and natural leadership abilities of other cadets. He was a superb judge of men, and those he noted with special favor at this time would come to the attention of the rest of the country three decades later as America entered World War I. Pershing's class of 1886 produced ten brigadier generals, fifteen major generals, and one General of the Armies—a total of twenty-six general officers, or over a third of the class. All told, the men Pershing knew during his four years at the academy furnished over a quarter of the 474 American generals in the war.[3]

Characteristics that Pershing later displayed as General of the Armies were already in evidence when he was a cadet. He worked hard. He was confident and possessed a strong intolerance for anyone he perceived as lazy. However, Pershing also gained a reputation for tardiness; every account of West Point days, written by men who knew him then, states that Pershing's overriding concern was seeking out the society of local ladies to join him for solitary walks along "flirtation lane." His classmates also considered him an odd mixture of vanity and shyness. He had a visceral negative reaction to being embarrassed. Among women, he was relaxed and even voluble, but when he was with other cadets he remained aloof. His classmates state that he was sociable and was considered a man among men, but he was never part of any clique or considered "one of the gang." One cadet, who later commanded a corps in World War I, said, "Pershing was never the kind of guy you walked up to and greeted with a slap on the back and a crude remark—twice."[4]

Despite his middling academic achievements, Pershing's military achievements at the academy entitled him to a high choice in selecting his branch of service and first assignment. He chose the Sixth Cavalry, mainly because it was still engaged in active operations, in the Southwest against the Apache Indians. He had intended to join the regiment immediately upon graduation, but as the Geronimo campaign was concluding, he decided to take his postgraduation leave and visit his family, now living in Lincoln, Nebraska.

Pershing's first posting was Fort Bayard, New Mexico, where he arrived just in time to go out on patrol in pursuit of the last of the Apache renegades, Chief Magnus. This first patrol was a shock to the new lieutenant, for it was quite obvious that many of the soldiers, including the troop's first sergeant, had liberally partaken of spirits prior to departing. But he also noted that the mules were all packed properly, the troopers' weapons were well maintained, and that they rode from dawn to dusk without complaint. Pershing's patrol never came across any hostile Apaches, as Magnus had returned to a reservation in Arizona, but the excursion taught Pershing how to plan and command an extended campaign in the field. It became one of many learning experiences he was to absorb during his four years in the Southwest.

During those years Pershing served in several posts and appears to have made a favorable impression on those above him. One commander said that new officers usually kept their mouths shut until they learned the basics of their profession from the ground up. But he said that Pershing was always different; "he was listened to by even the most senior officers almost from the day he arrived. He did not say much, but when he did it always went right to the meat of the problem."[5]

But Pershing was learning as well. Foremost among these lessons was how to handle enlisted men. In turn, his men discovered they were commanded by a man with real metal in his gut, who was not above enforcing discipline with his fists. For the most part, though, he respected his men and they repaid the feeling. Believing that the best way to inspire them was by setting the example, Pershing became almost fanatical about ensuring that he accomplished all of his assigned duties far above standard. He also took time to become an excellent marksman and was selected to defend his post's honor in a number of shooting competitions. His love affair with the rifle continued through the end of World War I, and it took a long time to convince Pershing that new artillery doctrine and massed machine guns had become a more important factor in war than well-trained marksmen.

As at West Point, Pershing was not all work. With the end of the Indian Campaigns, life in the far-flung Western outposts assumed a more leisurely pace. Pershing found ample time for extended hunting and fishing expeditions. Moreover, there seemed to be no shortage of social events to amuse young officers, and Pershing found that there were numerous opportunities for "spooning," a turn-of-the-century term for dating, and he went through an assortment of female admirers. Pershing also discovered that he had a natural affinity for poker, a talent that provided plentiful opportunities to supplement his salary. However, not wanting to get a reputation as a cardsharp, and troubled that he was beginning to drift off to sleep thinking about poker hands, he gave up the game.

To relieve the boredom of camp life and keep his men sharp, General Nelson Miles, the department commander, initiated a series of grueling training exercises. One favorite exercise had a troop of cavalry playing the part of raiders. They received a twelve- to twenty-four-hour head start, before a second troop was sent in pursuit. Pershing liked the maneuvers and considered them good training, despite the long days in the saddle. In one exercise, Pershing's troop covered 130 miles in less than forty hours. And the troop still finished with every horse and mule in good condition. Pershing beamed when Miles personally congratulated him on this achievement.

While assigned to Fort Wingate, Pershing was sent to arrest three white men trapped by over one hundred Zuni warriors intent on punishing them for killing three of their tribespeople. Pershing found the men under siege in a log house with the Zuni preparing a final rush to capture or kill them, the latter being their declared preference. Pershing convinced the Zuni to cease fire and allow him to arrest the men, whereupon, he explained, they would surely be tried and hanged. Alone, Pershing entered the log house, and told the men that if they did not agree to being arrested he would depart and leave them to the Zuni's "tender mercies." The men saw reason and Pershing led them out on a buckboard, wondering if the Indians would jump the entire party. When he returned, the post commander congratulated him on his peaceful handling of a touchy situation. In the end, however, one of the prisoners escaped from the post stockade, and civilian authorities failed to convict the other two.

On November 23, 1890, the Sixth Cavalry received orders to move to South Dakota. At the time, a new movement was spreading rapidly among the Plains Indians. Known as the Ghost Dancers, this group claimed that any Indian who wore special magical shirts and performed the Ghost Dance would become immune to the white man's bullets. In November 3,000 Sioux Indians left the Rosebud Pine Ridge Reservation and fortified themselves on a high mesa, where they awaited the arrival of an Indian messiah who would lead them in a great war to take back their lands. As other Indians began leaving the reservation, civilian authorities lost control of the region and Miles received orders to take charge.

According to Pershing, Miles was a fine soldier with much experience fighting Indians who also understood and felt sympathy for the natives and their plight. Even before being assigned to the command, Miles had made protestations to Washington on the

Indians' behalf and had received permission to feed starving tribes out of Army stores. Realizing that if the great multitude of roving Indian bands were able to concentrate, they would constitute a significant military threat, Miles planned his campaign so as to isolate and then overwhelm each Indian band in turn. From the start, Miles understood that many of the Indians were waiting on the actions of their great chief, Sitting Bull, the man who wiped out General George Custer's Seventh Cavalry. In an effort to remove the famous chief, Miles sent Buffalo Bill Cody to induce him to surrender. When that failed, he sent a platoon of Indian scouts to arrest him. A firefight ensued and the aged Indian chief was killed during the melee, further enraging the hostile tribes.

Miles' tact, knowledge, and ability had temporarily halted the spread of the Ghost Dancer movement, but the key to turning back those already involved lay in forcing the Indians who had fled the Pine Ridge Reservation to return. To do this, Miles established a strong cordon of cavalry around the Indian's fortified mesa, of which Pershing's troop was a part. Patrolling along the Cheyenne River Valley for the next several weeks, he and his men were almost constantly in the saddle. The temperatures were almost always below zero, and there were several deadly blizzards during the operation, which constantly challenged Pershing's leadership ability. Though Pershing's force encountered little combat, a large group of fleeing Indians under Chief Big Foot was captured by the nearby Seventh Cavalry Regiment. The Seventh Cavalry's commander, Colonel Forsyth, ordered the group to be disarmed, and when one of the Indians resisted, a struggle ensued. By the end of what became known as the Battle of Wounded Knee, thirty cavalry officers and men and two hundred Indians had been killed.

The battle came as a shock to Miles, as he had just convinced the other chiefs on the mesa to give up and return to the reservation. When the chiefs heard about Wounded Knee, they reversed their decision. It took two more weeks of careful negotiating before Miles could convince them to surrender. Throughout this period,

Pershing and his troopers stayed out on patrol, as part of Miles' dual strategy of showing overwhelming force, combined with massively increasing the amount of food available to the starving tribes, if they agreed to his terms. Despite the hardships and what he had undeniably learned about commanding men under arduous circumstances, the one thing Pershing later wrote about this campaign was his own wonderment at how much food he had eaten on a daily basis.

The Ghost Dancer movement ended early in 1891 and concluded the Indian Wars. With the onset of peace, Pershing began looking for new challenges. While visiting his family in Lincoln, he applied for the position of military instructor at the University of Nebraska. The idea of intellectual improvement by socializing with the faculty appealed to Pershing, who found himself bored with the limited intellectual fare available on isolated outposts. So, with no prospects of active field service, Pershing applied for and was appointed the commandant of cadets at the University of Nebraska.

Pershing took over a foundering corps of cadets. Although most university students were required to be part of the corps, they took to it with varying degrees of interest, running from low to nonexistent. Pershing started with the fundamentals, which to him meant discipline. As a first step, he instilled in his cadets the concept of attendance, which many students were shocked to discover meant actually showing up for drill. Pershing was quick to punish, but equally liberal with rewards. He also reorganized the corps following the model of West Point, so that cadet corporals came from the sophomore class, sergeants from the juniors, and officers from the seniors. It gave more cadets a taste of authority and responsibility than would otherwise have been the case under the old system.

It might be expected that college students would rebel at Pershing's heavy-handed discipline, but surprisingly, they reveled in it. The cadets soon came to idolize Pershing. As one recalled: "We all tried to walk like Pershing, talk like Pershing, and look like Pershing. His personality and strength of character dominated us. Every inch of him was a soldier. In all my life I have never seen a man with such poise, dignity and personality. Whether in uniform or not, he attracted attention wherever he went. But he was always affable and interesting to talk to, and popular with students and professors."[6]

Pershing's cadets reached a pinnacle of performance when he entered them into 1892 National Drill Competition, held in Omaha that year. In the division set aside for first-time entrants, Pershing's cadets easily took first place and won $1,500. It was the turning point of the program, and the victory was greeted on campus with the same enthusiasm that today's universities give to major football bowl wins. Afterward, the cadets, on their own initiative, created an elite drill corps, named the Varsity Rifles. By 1895, it was being called the Pershing Rifles, the first of scores of drill teams that bear that designation today.

Not all of Pershing's time was spent on the corps. He prevailed upon the university's chancellor, James H. Canfield, to allow him to supplement his meager army salary by teaching several classes in mathematics. Canfield was impressed with Pershing from the beginning, but noticed that with Pershing, time was either put to practical use or wasted. There were reports that Pershing was wasting too much time in local saloons. To fill his spare time more effectively, Canfield suggested that Pershing enroll in the university's nascent law school. According to Canfield's daughter, the famous novelist Dorothy Canfield Fisher, who would later become one of Pershing's great friends, "Pershing had a reputation for not being the most sober member of society. My father knew that a full-blooded young man of that age really wouldn't have enough to do to keep him out of mischief if all he had was training the cadet battalion and a few math classes."[7]

Since the idea of studying the law had always appealed to Pershing, he readily accepted the chancellor's invitation, and received his cherished law degree in June 1893. With his degree in hand, Pershing went to discuss his options with a former law classmate, who later became Pershing's best friend and confidant, Charles Dawes. Dawes was a struggling new lawyer in Lincoln and, although successful later in life, eventually becoming the Vice President of the United States, he was having a hard time in the late 1890s. Both men would often meet for lunch at Dom Cameron's lunch counter, where "the food was good and, what was more to the point, the price was low."

At one of these meetings, Pershing gave Dawes an assessment of his prospects. After over a decade in the army he was still only a lieutenant, and his income was meager. As Pershing saw it, at best he could hope to retire as a major in another couple of decades. Moreover, he was not elated about the prospect of ending his days with few recognized achievements and living close to penury. He asked Dawes if he would consider forming a law partnership. Dawes said no. "Better lawyers than either you or I can ever hope to be are starving in Nebraska," he warned. "I'd try the Army for awhile yet. Your pay may be small, but it comes regularly." Pershing took the advice. Still, throughout his life there were many periods, even after making general, when he had second thoughts and considered leaving the army for the law. As for Dawes, he remained a lifelong friend and gave Pershing and the United States invaluable assistance during World War I.

In spring 1895, Pershing's tour of duty at the university drew to a close. Canfield wrote of him, "He is the most energetic, active, industrious, competent, and successful officer I have ever known." As for Pershing, he considered the experience one of the most profitable of his life and later wrote, "It would be an excellent thing if every officer in the army could have contact in this way with the youth which forms our citizenship in peace and our armies in war. It would broaden the officer's outlook and better fit him for his duties in the army, especially in time of war."

Pershing's next assignment was the all-black Tenth Cavalry—the famed Buffalo Soldiers. His stay there was short and rather uneventful. For its effects on his personal and professional development, it is memorable for two main reasons. First, Pershing lived during a period of ingrained racism. The belief that blacks were inferior was not something maintained only by isolated bigots. It was part of the cultural mainstream. Pershing, like most white officers who served in all black regiments, soon discovered that blacks were some of the best soldiers the army produced. All they asked of any officer was that he show them the same respect that any soldier in a white regiment received. Pershing never had any trouble with that request and considered it a privilege to be assigned to the regiment. It was his service in an all black regiment which led to his famous moniker, "Blackjack," given to him by West Point cadets after he left the Tenth Cavalry and was assigned to the academy. It was a nickname not meant to flatter.

The second important impact of his time in the Tenth was that Pershing's professional prospects advanced when General Miles visited the Tenth Cavalry and decided to go on a multiday hunting expedition, with Pershing as his escort. During the trip, Pershing so impressed Miles that, when Pershing took leave in Washington, D.C., a few months later, Miles had him assigned to his personal staff. His tour in Washington was a short one, but it did bring him one contact that was critical to his later advancement—Theodore Roosevelt. He met Roosevelt at a dinner and the two men hit it off immediately. At the time, Roosevelt was New York City's police commissioner, but he still had fond recollections of the time he spent in the West and appreciated being able to share them with a man who understood what he was talking about. Pershing later wrote, "Here was a man, I thought, whose personality and vigor would carry him a long way. Marked by a decided individuality, whether as police commissioner, Rough Rider, or president, he was the type one never forgets."

While in Washington, the commandant of cadets at West Point asked him to serve as a tactical officer. Pershing, having turned down several requests in the past to take the same assignment, in favor of staying with troops, saw the offer as a chance to escape Washington and desk duty, reversed himself, and accepted. It turned out to be the biggest mistake of his professional life—and thankfully short-lived. Upon arriving at West Point in 1897, Pershing lost no time making himself possibly the most hated tactical officer in academy history. Though he had enforced a strict code of discipline at the University of Nebraska, it had been tempered with humor, understanding, kindness, and flexibility. For reasons yet undiscovered, none of these qualities were in evidence in his treatment of the West Point cadets. By common agreement, Pershing was the poster boy of a martinet, and the cadets rebelled. Their attempts at rebellion and demonstrations of how much they despised Pershing only led to harsher punishments, which fed a vicious cycle.

There may have been only one bright side to Pershing's tenure at West Point. As terrible as the experience was, Pershing learned there was a point beyond which one cannot profitably push men. In any organization men will only accept discipline they consider just and reasonable and will not submit willingly to harsh measures for which they can see no purpose. Trying to impose a higher level of discipline on men who do not see the point runs up against the law of diminishing returns. Never again would Pershing make so grievous a mistake in human relationships. In the future, his men would never have the same affection for him that the cadets at Nebraska did, but neither would they feel cold hatred for him, like the cadets at West Point. The troops' relationship with Pershing became more neutral, which is probably best summed up in the word *respect*.[8]

As Pershing endured his tribulations at West Point, the country, incensed by sensationalized media stories of Spanish atrocities in Cuba, was edging ever closer to war with Spain. If there was going to be a war, Pershing was determined to be part of it. Because the leadership at West Point refused to release him, he took leave to visit a Nebraska friend in Washington who was now Assistant Secretary of War, George D. Meiklejohn. After some persuading, Meiklejohn agreed to assign Pershing back to the buffalo soldiers of the Tenth Cavalry as the quartermaster, a job the regimental commander had previously offered him. Pershing would have preferred a troop command, but he was not going to refuse any assignment that would get him to the war zone. In the margin of his unpublished autobiography, Pershing had scribbled, "My action in going directly to Meiklejohn was not all in keeping with accepted army procedure then, and would not be today, but with our country at war I felt it excusable."

CHAPTER 2

The Splendid Little War

THE SPANISH-AMERICAN WAR WAS A BRIEF BUT INTENSE
conflict that deprived Spain of most of its remaining colonies and
placed them in the hands of the United States. It was precipitated
by a prolonged campaign of yellow journalism that portrayed the
Spanish treatment of Cubans, which was never gentle, as barbaric
and inhuman. Moreover, it blamed Spain for the accidental destruction of the U.S.S. *Maine* in Havana Harbor. Two great naval
battles, one in the Philippines and the other off the coast of Cuba,
and the Army's assault on San Juan Hill, decided this unequal military struggle. When it was over, Spain had been reduced to a third-
rate power, and the United States had taken its first step on the
global stage. In a letter to his friend Theodore Roosevelt, John Hay,
the American ambassador to Britain, called it a "splendid little
war." However, it was anything but splendid for the men who endured weltering heat, disease, and deadly Spanish fire.

Pershing joined the Tenth Cavalry Regiment at Chickamauga, Georgia on May 5, 1898, only to find complete chaos. Nothing had been done to prepare the regiment for war and even the basics of requisitioning blankets, food, and ammunition had not been attended to. Delving into these pressing tasks, Pershing soon brought order. For the soldiers of the Tenth Cavalry, Pershing's arrival was a blessing, since it was thanks to him that they began receiving regular meals.

However, there was one problem the unit faced that was beyond Pershing's ability to resolve.

> The people of the south had not seen much regular army since reconstruction days and were somewhat inclined to look askance at us. A friendly attitude, however, soon became the rule and very soon our officers were being entertained in private homes in the most hospitable fashion. But their feeling toward the colored troops was different from that in the north and some of the men resented it. Barbers refused to serve our men and in one shop the proprietor put up a sign, "N***** not wanted" One evening one of our recruits entered the shop and demanded a shave, which was refused with an insulting remark, whereupon the soldier stepped outside and firing his pistol through the window killed the barber.

After this incident, the regimental commander had the enlisted soldiers confined to camp for the duration of their stay in Georgia.

Orders to move to Tampa for embarkation to Cuba came at the end of May, and Pershing was soon embroiled with the preparations and conduct of the move. If Chickamauga was chaotic, Tampa was in crisis. No one, it seemed, had done any prior planning for the concentration of troops or given any thought as to how this tiny hamlet would handle the thousands of soldiers descending upon it. All that the planners in Washington had cared about was that the town had several piers and was close to Cuba. Pershing and other quartermasters were forced to take things into their own hands. They formed details to break into trains, trucks, and warehouses, and appropriated anything they thought their units might require.

While Pershing did his best to get the Tenth Cavalry supplies, they received discouraging news. General Nelson Miles would not command the invasion force. Instead the command fell to the corpulent General William Shafter, who had never commanded more than a regiment. Miles was refused the command because he was known to have political ambitions, and President William McKinley, worried about the 1900 elections, wanted to avoid facing a victorious and popular general in the polls. The lesson was not lost on Pershing, who assiduously avoided the complications of politics during the rest of his military career. Later, when President Woodrow Wilson had to choose the commander for the American Expeditionary Force (AEF) in World War I, he ultimately selected Pershing precisely because he was known to have no political ambitions.

On June 7, the Tenth Cavalry embarked on the *Leona,* as part of the First Cavalry Division, commanded by the famous former Confederate Cavalry commander, General "Fighting Joe" Wheeler.[1] After several days of delay and ultimately useless circling to avoid a Spanish Fleet that was, contrary to widespread belief, already effectively bottled up by the U.S. Navy, the *Leona* arrived off the coast of Cuba. While the amphibious assault faced no Spanish resistance, it almost defeated itself—soldiers burdened with useless equipment drowned in the surf, while panicked horses and mules swam out to sea, taking critical supplies with them.

Eventually 17,000 soldiers struggled ashore and prepared a support base for an advance on Santiago, where the Spanish Army was waiting in fortified positions. Pershing did not land with the troops and was chagrined about missing the unit's first minor combat engagement. Instead, he was sent with the *Leona* to pick up an estimated 3,000 Cuban fighters who were waiting to join the American cause. Unfortunately, what Pershing found did not live up to the billing:

> [The 1,000] we took aboard were a rag-tag, bob-tailed, poorly armed, and hungry lot in appearance anything but an effective fighting force. We had to give them food and all we could get out of the hold at the time was hardbread and sugar, which they ate ravenously . . . we got little or no help during the campaign from this or any band of Cuban *insurrectos*.

When Pershing got back to the landing beaches, the situation was still chaotic, but the army had consolidated a beachhead and pushed a couple of miles inland. There had been a short but sharp fight at Las Guasimas, but the conscripted Spaniards' hearts were not in the fight, and they retired to their main fortifications at Santiago, obviously unwilling to contest the American advance. General Shafter did not rush the attack, as he wanted to offload as much of the supplies as possible, while giving his commanders time to acclimate themselves and conduct reconnaissance missions. But he was also aware that too much of a delay meant disaster. It was already late June and in a few weeks the mosquitoes would be out in full force and the army would find itself decimated by malaria.

On July 1, Shafter finally gave the order to attack, Pershing remembers the day as ideal:

> . . . the air soft and balmy . . . our division had bivouacked near El Pozo, about two miles east of San Juan Hill. The camp was stirring at daybreak and our men were eager to enter what for most of them was to be their first battle. They stood about in small groups oppo-

site their places in column, impatient for the order to advance. From the low ridge near the trail we could see the lines of the enemy entrenchments and the blockhouses along the heights of San Juan. Beyond could be seen the successive lines of defense and behind them arose the spires and towers of the city we were preparing to invest. To the northeast, overlooking all approaches, the stone fort and smaller blockhouses of the enemy outpost at El Caney were outlined against the sky.

At 6:30 A.M. the first American artillery battery opened fire. By 8:30 A.M. there was a lively artillery duel well underway. The slow-firing, obsolete American guns were mostly ineffective, as the range was too great, and the Americans were soon enshrouded in smoke, which both gave away their location and obscured their view of the enemy positions. The Spanish used smokeless powder, which did not betray their positions, and gave them a distinct advantage in the artillery fight. The only modern artillery the Americans possessed was a quick firing European battery that millionaire Jacob Astor had purchased for the army at his own expense.[2] The battery was commanded by Captain Peyton March and was recognized as the best and most effective artillery unit in Cuba. In his unpublished autobiography, Pershing fails to mention the unit, which may have been a reflection of the troubles that arose between the two men when March was army chief of staff and Pershing commanded the American army in France during World War I.

At 8:30 A.M. the Tenth Cavalry received the order to advance along the El Pozo–Santiago road, cross the Aguadores River and then deploy to the right of the American battle line. The approach was torturous, narrow, and flanked on both sides by dense jungle. Moreover, by the time the advance began the sun was beating down and it was not long before men began dropping from the heat. At first there was only an occasional bullet nipping the leaves around the column, but as the soldiers approached the river, a U.S. army observation balloon came forward and hovered 200 yards above the regiment. The glimmering white balloon drew the fire of every Spanish gun, and men began to fall. As the regiment withstood "a veritable hail of shot and shell," the balloon commander yelled down to inform the men below that the enemy was firing on them. This announcement was met with a hail of heart-felt epithets, and the men on the ground brought the balloon down.

As the fire grew in intensity, the Seventy-First New York Volunteers broke. Some ran back down the trail, but most just fell to the ground where they were and refused to move. The regulars of the Sixth and Tenth Cavalry, along with the Rough Riders, stepped over them and on them, and continued to advance. The cavalry units crossed the river and moved to the right, while the infantry deployed to the left. When the soldiers broke free of the jungle they immediately came under terrible fire from the fortified positions on the ridge. Their only option was to lie down in the tall grass and hide while they waited for the final order to assault.

As often happens during a military movement, there had been a break in contact between units, and one of the Tenth Cavalry's squadrons had strayed. Pershing went back to retrieve it. Along the way, he saw the division commander, General Wheeler, sitting on his horse in the middle of the river as bullets plucked the water around him. Pershing was shocked to find him at the front—the general had been diagnosed with malaria and confined to bed by his doctors. He moved closer, saluted, and was about to comment on the danger the general faced in such an exposed position when a shell hit the water and exploded between the two men. Wheeler returned the salute and casually remarked that the shelling seemed quite lively. Pershing decided not to say anything and turned to find his lost squadron. He never forgot the lesson of that day— Wheeler was exposed to danger because his division was. A fighting general did no less.

Pershing eventually found the missing squadron and brought it into line with the rest of the regiment. When he got back to the line, he found the accurate Spanish fire galling, as casualties mounted. For over thirty minutes the regiment lay in the grass until they could no longer simply remain idle to be shot to pieces. It was time to either advance or retreat. However, retreat down the crowded road was impossible, and defeat was unthinkable. Finally, the order came—advance. In a single wave, the cavalry troopers swept forward.

It was hard to keep order in the tall grass and with volunteers mixed with regulars, black soldiers with Rough Riders. But Pershing was fiercely proud of his soldiers: "The men took cover only when ordered to do so and exposed themselves fearlessly," he later wrote. This was Pershing's baptism by fire, and revealed a trait he was to be known for in the Philippines and during World War I— no matter what he felt inside, Pershing always appeared to be utterly fearless. One West Pointer watching him place soldiers in position while under heavy fire wrote that, "He was as cool as a bowl of cracked ice." His commander, Colonel Theodore Baldwin, sent him a note later saying, "I have been in many fights in the Civil War, but on my word you are the coolest and bravest man I ever saw under fire in my life."[3]

As the advance continued, Pershing describes the action:

It was a hot fight . . . the converging artillery fire made life worth nothing. We waded the river to our armpits and formed line in an opening in dense undergrowth facing our objective, the San Juan block-house, all the while exposed to volley firing from front, left front & left flank, and you know what it means to be uncertain as to the position of the enemy.

On the dusky troopers trudged, their number being gradually diminished until they reached the open in front of the position when they advanced by rushes almost half way—then went the balance with a charge.

Spanish small arm fire is terrible. . . . Men in the third & fourth lines were in as great danger as those nearer—indeed less casualties occurred close to the entrenchments.[4]

Despite the troopers' bravery, the battle remained in doubt. The closer they pushed to the summit, the more deadly the Spanish fire. It was not until Lieutenant John Henry Parker managed to drag his Gatling guns down the road and set them up within rifle shot of the Spanish that the tide finally turned. Parker's battery lost half its men, but still swept San Juan Hill with a devastating fire. Slammed with 36,000 rounds a minute from Parker's guns, Spanish morale collapsed, and the enemy soldiers streamed to the rear. Pershing and the cavalry troopers rushed and then swarmed over the summit. They took San Juan Hill. Pershing remembered the moment: "In the elation that followed this achievement men cheered, shook hands with each other and threw their arms about each other, and generally behaved wildly regardless of rank . . . a colored trooper gently raised the head of a wounded Spanish lieutenant and gave him the last drop of water from his canteen."

The soldiers quickly prepared their hard-won positions for defense against an expected Spanish counterattack, but Pershing was dismayed to hear Colonel Leonard Wood, the Rough Rider commander, suggest the hill could not be held and that he was going to recommend a retreat. Pershing took "decided issue with that view" and argued that it would be a serious mistake. Other officers joined the debate and, while the junior officers wanted to hold the ground they had spent so much blood taking, senior officers supported a retreat. The matter was taken to General Joseph Wheeler, who immediately quashed any notion of a pull-back. He was not called "Fighting Joe" for nothing.

The next morning the Spanish did counterattack, but the Americans easily beat them back. For the next two weeks, American troops conducted modified siege operations, as they tightened the loop around Santiago, and the Spanish negotiated their surrender. As the surrender negotiations dragged on, malaria laid the American Army low. During this period, Pershing was given the position of regimental adjutant and took command of three troops of cavalry, as their officers had been successively bowled over by disease. Though suffering from malaria himself, Pershing also retained his position of quartermaster, which necessitated frequent grueling trips through a quagmire of mud back to the main supply base.

On one trip back to the rear supply points, he heard a great commotion in the darkness ahead. Pershing came abreast of another wagon mired up to its hubs in mud. The driver "was urging his team forward with all the skill, including the forceful language of a born mule-skinner." Years later that wagon driver and Pershing were having dinner and the driver asked eagerly if Pershing remembered what he said. Pershing answered, "Mr. President [Roosevelt], that I cannot repeat in the presence of the ladies."[5] Colonel Baldwin later commented on Pershing's performance as quartermaster, "You did some tall rustling, and if you had not, we would have starved, as none of the others were able or strong enough to do it." By all rights, Pershing should not have been able to do so either, as he took on the jobs of five men, while shaking off the effects of malaria by sheer willpower.

<hr />

The surrender of Santiago took place on July 17, 1898, and it came not a moment too soon. By the beginning of August, over 75 percent of the American force was down with malaria, and evacuation became imperative. Despite being wracked with chills and fever, Pershing continued to command three companies, keep up with his quartermaster duties, and act as the regimental adjutant. It was a back-breaking work load for a healthy man. For Pershing, suffering from malaria, it nearly wrecked his health permanently.

On August 14, the Tenth Cavalry finally embarked and sailed for Montauk Point, New York, to rest and rehabilitate. Upon arrival in New York, Pershing was told that a million dollars worth of property charged to his name as unit quartermaster was unaccounted for and that he was personally responsible for the debt. The army auditor also explained that his pay would be cut off until he could account for all of the material. A young lieutenant, James G. Harbord, came to Pershing's rescue. Harbord noted that many of the returning troops had more equipment then they were supposed to have. He collected it, inventoried it, and told Pershing that it looked like about a million dollars worth of government property. Harbord had the accounts updated to satisfy the auditors, while Pershing took special note of this young officer.

The Spanish-American War may have been short, but it was also demanding and brutal. Pershing took away from the conflict a number of lessons about himself as well as about the nature of war. He was justifiably proud of how he had stood up to his first test under fire, and from that point on knew that he would never be troubled by the dangers of mortal combat. His position as quartermaster was also critical to his development as a great field commander. Like Grant, who was a regimental quartermaster in the Mexican-American War, Pershing learned the truth behind the old adage "amateurs talk tactics, professionals talk logistics." Unless the supply needs of an army were well thought out and firmly established, successful action was impossible no matter how brave the troops. When the United States entered World War I, Pershing would spend over a year building up his logistical base before he committed sizable American forces to combat. The main American attack in World War I may have been a long time in coming, but when it did, Pershing ensured it would hit like a battering ram.

CHAPTER 3

The Philippines Insurgency

AFTER THE SPANISH-AMERICAN WAR, PERSHING SERVED A short tour in Washington, but despite a friend's advice to stay in the city where he was most likely to make general as the head of an army department, he soon began angling for a transfer to the Philippines.

The Philippines became an American possession at the end of the Spanish-American War and was the crown jewel of the new American empire. However, it was a troublesome jewel, for along with a new territory, America inherited an insurrection. In 1899, stiff fighting broke out between Philippine insurgents, led by Emilio Aguinaldo, and the American army. Both sides waged a ruthless battle until Aguinaldo was defeated in 1902. Of the thirty American generals who fought in the Philippines, twenty-six of them had learned their business fighting Indians. They brought many of the same tactics that effectively crushed the Indian nations to bear on the Filipino insurgents. At the same time, though, the Americans adopted a policy of pacification, which included health programs, public sanitation, and universal education, which convinced many Filipinos they had more to gain through cooperation than through resistance.

The Philippines was where Pershing could find combat, and he wanted to be part of it. Besides, combat duty was always good for a soldier's reputation and advancement, and Pershing was ambitious. In late 1899, he got his wish and took passage to the Philippines.

Brutal battles for control of Luzon and the northern Philippines were still being bitterly waged when Pershing arrived in Manila. But instead of joining that fight, Pershing was sent to Mindanao, the southernmost major island in the Philippine archipelago. Mindanao was plagued not so much by an insurrection as by a problem regarding the Moro. The Moros are ethnically indistinguishable from other Filipinos, but, unlike the Filipinos, who are Catholic, they are almost all Muslim. The Moro also were known to raid mountain tribes or even their fellow tribesmen. They did this with primitive armaments, mostly ancient weapons stolen from the Spanish, and their weapon of choice was a blade, which Pershing later described:

> The pride of the Moro, however, is in his *kris,* his *compilan,* his *barong,* or his *head knife,* the four classes of cutting weapons with which he is most familiar. Many of these arms have been tested in tribal wars and handed down from generation to generation. Much as the Moro appreciates the value of money, he will not part with his cherished weapons, the greatest inheritance in his mind that his forefathers have bequeathed him. . . . These keen edged weapons of warfare were well calculated to do effective work in hand-to hand combat when wielded by a

skillful fighter . . . some experts can cut a human in two with a single blow.

Much like the tribes the U.S. Army is fighting in Afghanistan and Iraq today, the Moros were ruled by tribal chiefs, call *dattos,* who led groups of several hundred persons, and respected no central authority. Upon his arrival in Mindanao, Pershing quickly realized that his effectiveness rested on his ability to understand the people with whom he was dealing. He began studying the Moro language and culture—one of the few Americans who bothered doing so. He recorded his findings:

> The Moro is of a peculiar make-up as to character, though the reason is plain when considered, first, that he is a savage; second that he is a Malay; and third, that he is a Mohammedan. The almost infinite combination of superstitions, prejudices and suspicions blended into his character make him a difficult person to handle until finally understood. In order to control him other than by brute force, one must first win his implicit confidence, nor is this as difficult as it would seem; but once accomplished one can accordingly by patient and continuous effort, largely guide and direct his thoughts and actions. He is jealous of his religion, but he knows very little of its teachings. The observance of a few rites and rituals is about all that is required to satisfy him that he is a good Mohammedan.[1]

What was not lost on Pershing was the fact that the Moros were a dangerous force and that one day the entire region would require pacification.

The most disturbing aspect of dealing with the Moros was the tendency of their young men to become *juramentados,* or oath-takers. Unfortunately for American soldiers and most other Filipinos, the oath was to kill as many infidels as possible in order to be guaranteed a place in paradise, when eventually the *juramentado* was inevitably killed himself. These fanatics would walk down a road full of civilians and then, without warning, draw a large blade and start hacking at any Christian within reach. To the chagrin of many soldiers in the vicinity of one of these attacks, the *juramentados* were either drugged or in such states of ecstasy that army-issue .38 revolvers made no impression on them. Pershing's autobiography relates the story of one officer who emptied his revolver into a charging *juramentado* but was still hacked to pieces. The army's .45 pistol, whose round stuck like a sledgehammer, was specifically designed to stop charging *juramentados*.

━━━

Initially, Pershing's duties remained limited to administrative functions. That changed when General George W. Davis assumed control of the region and realized that Pershing was the only one who understood the Moros enough to have any chance of pacifying them without excessive violence. Davis made it a habit to consult with Pershing on Moro matters and eventually told Pershing, "I am going to send you to Iligan [the center of most violent Moro activity in the region]. I'll give you two troops of your regiment and three companies of infantry. Do everything possible to get in touch with the Moros in central Mindanao and make friends with them."

By now Pershing, after fifteen years of active service, was a captain, administratively assigned to the newly constituted Fifteenth Cavalry Regiment. This was a green unit and when Pershing asked its commander the state of the first arrivals in the Philippines, he was told, "I have a hundred horses that have never seen a soldier, a hundred soldiers who have never seen a horse, and a bunch of officers who have never seen either."

Pershing lost no time on his new assignment, but he was far from pleased when he saw conditions at Iligan, which he judged in need of a firm hand. He made his first impression on his new troopers by entering the mess hall and tossing every pot and pan he judged below accepted cleanliness standards at the heads of the cooks. On his next trip to the mess hall, he commented to his sergeant major that the cooking equipment looked better and inquired as to why the cooks were wearing helmets in such heat.

After restoring a degree of military discipline, Pershing turned his attention to befriending the local Moros. As a first step, he visited local Moros and engaged them in conversation. He asked them about their crops, their kids, and the health of their *dattos*. He also began making purchases from the local Moros of whatever items they had to sell, always paying a bit over the market price, but not enough so they thought him a fool. Moreover, he began building roads and schools, and hiring the necessary labor from among the Moros. Unable to fathom the reason why the new American commander wanted to help his people, the local sultan, Manibilang, sent his son to meet Pershing. Pershing greeted him warmly and sent him off with an invitation for Manibilang to come and visit. After a few letters, the great-man of the local Moros consented to visit.

The sultan stayed for three days and peppered Pershing with questions during multihour conferences, each of which stands as a testament to Pershing's endurance and patience, as the same concerns were voiced over and over again.

Will you compel us to wear hats?
Will you force our women to wear skirts?
Will you try and force us to eat pork?

Pershing addressed many of the chief's qualms, but carefully avoided questions of Moro society like slavery and multiple wives, planning to tackle those thorny issues when Moro-American relations were more peaceful. Unfortunately, all of Pershing's early attempts to build relationships with the Moros ran into the same wall. The *dottos* just could not believe that the Americans wanted nothing but friendship and peace from them, and that, in return, the Americans would bring prosperity to the region. There was nothing in the Moro's experience or historical tradition that allowed them to comprehend such altruism. But Pershing stuck to his message, conference after conference, and for endless hours. Slowly he made progress.

When the Sultan Manibilang finally took his leave, he announced that he could live with the Americans. After that, other *dattos* began visiting and asking for an interview with Pershing, who noted, "they all had a particular desire to get rich." He also began a letter-writing campaign with all of the *dattos* in the region to keep them posted on developments and to solicit their advice. In time, he had made such progress with local *dattos* that the Sultan Manibilang made the unprecedented move of inviting Pershing to his camp. Fearing Moro treachery, many thought Pershing rash to accept the invitation. When he announced he was forgoing an infantry escort and taking only an interpreter, they thought him a fool. Undeterred, Pershing went unescorted and his trust paid off, as other dattos soon began to invite him to their camps. As he later noted:

> From that time, Manibilang was not only a warm personal friend of mine but an earnest advocate of friendly relations between Americans and Moros. In the months to come he rendered much valuable assistance in dissuading other dattos from opposition. With the exception of a few groups, the Lanao Moros in general, largely through his influence, became friendly. The word spread of the good business that could be done at Iligan and the security afforded all Moros there and the number of people who came to market steadily increased.

To the Moros, Pershing was the United States, and they particularly appreciated that, when Pershing promised something, he delivered. The Moros recognized that the word of Captain Pershing could be taken to the bank. Troublemakers still persisted, but Pershing had a way of dealing with the problem that other Americans had not even considered. He let the Moros handle it for him, and here we see the ruthless side of Pershing's nature, but a ruthlessness his Moro friends appreciated. As he explained in a letter home to his mother: "I have many very strong personal friends among the Moros. Some of them will do anything for me. If I should say: 'Go and kill this man or that,' the next day they appear in camp with his head."[2]

While Pershing was making progress at Iligan, the Moros on the southern side of the lake were becoming ever more troublesome. They continually attacked American patrols, and casualties mounted. Determined to end the violence, Colonel Baldwin, the area commander, took a strong force into the jungle and marched on one of their fortified posts, called *cottas*. The Moros built these *cottas* so solidly that they had resisted the Spanish for over 300 years. *Cottas* varied in size and strength, but even the weakest had walls twenty feet high and almost as thick. They were surrounded by moats, which were often twenty meters wide and thirty meters deep, usually filled with sharpened bamboo sticks.

Baldwin approached the massive *cotta* at Pandapatan and after an hour's bombardment ordered a direct assault. The net result of this order was the loss of fifty American soldiers with no visible effect on the *cotta*. Baldwin pulled back and prepared for a stronger and better coordinated assault the next morning. But during the night the Moros escaped into the jungle. Baldwin burned down the *cotta*, but it was not much to show for the loss of fifty U.S. soldiers. The following day, Pershing was summoned by the department commander, General Adna Chaffee, and given precise orders: He was to go to the newly constructed Camp Vickers (named for the first soldier killed in the attack on Pandapatan), where Colonel Baldwin would remain in command of the camp, but where Pershing would be in charge of Moro affairs. Baldwin saw this exactly for what it was—a vote of no confidence.

Baldwin and Pershing were old friends and the two often went out on inspection tours and other excursions together, during which Baldwin rarely lost an opportunity to try to win Pershing over to his way of dealing with the Moros. But Pershing had his own proven methods and he resisted Baldwin's entreaties to attack, relying instead on what had worked so well at Iligan. When Baldwin insisted, Chaffee prevailed on the War Department to promote him to general and order him back to the United States. Pershing was left at Camp Vickers, in command of what amounted to a detached regiment.

+—=—+

Pershing's methods worked only up to a point. Although he made many Moro friends on the south side of Lake Lanao, there were still a few *dottos* that resisted his appeals. These *dottos* built a strong position around a series of *cottas* located at Maciu, Bayan, and Bacoclod. Four months of dealing peaceably with these rebels yielded no results. In fact, things got worse, and Moro attacks on isolated outposts and sniping upon Camp Vickers increased. Still looking for a peaceful solution, Pershing did not seek retribution for any of these outrages. In time, previously friendly Moro tribes began to question Pershing's will and authority and a number of Pershing's fellow officers shared these sentiments. Many believed Pershing no longer had the stomach to lead men into a fight, while some thought he might even be a closet pacifist.

Realizing he was losing prestige among the Moros, Pershing determined that it was time to act. He brought a plan to his new commander, General Samuel Sumner, who quickly incorporated it into a larger offensive he was planning in order to pacify the area.

On September 18, 1902, Pershing marched on Maciu with 700 men. He sent a message to the two hostile sultans whose followers manned the *cottas,* inviting them to visit and confer with him. The reply came, "We do not want to meet with you anywhere except at Maciu. We shall be waiting for you at Maciu." It was an ominous warning.

Unwilling to provoke the hostile Moros while there was still a chance for peace, Pershing had decided not to send out patrols to recon his route. So, he was surprised when, well short of Maciu, he ran into an ambush. Displaying his trademark steel nerves under fire, Pershing calmly ordered his force out of the kill zone and deployed his artillery to pound the Moro positions into splinters. With no way to get at Pershing's artillery, the Moros retreated back to their main *cottas* at Maciu. Pershing continued his march, but was soon defeated by the terrain. The jungle proved an impossible obstacle, and Pershing was unable to move his artillery and supplies. Unwilling to sacrifice American lives in an unsupported infantry attack, Pershing retreated.

The galling taunts of the Moros followed him all the way back to his base, despite Pershing periodically stopping to unlimber his artillery and firing at the jeerers to "ruin their fun." For centuries the Moros had resisted every Spanish encroachment and could not fathom that Pershing would be any more successful. After all, he was not near as ruthless as the Spanish had been.

Ruthless, Pershing may not have been, but he was determined. A week later, Pershing was on the march to Maciu again, but this time he brought a detachment of engineers. He built a road as he went. It was not a good road, but it sufficed. By October 1, the Americans were in front of Maciu. Seeing the massed artillery, over half of the sultan's fighters thought better of their oath to fight to the death and fled. Pershing thought it a good idea to encourage the rest to do the same. Understanding that this struggle was about prestige and not body count, Pershing knew his purposes would be served just as well if he entered a deserted *cotta* and burned it to the ground as they would be if he fought a bloody fight to achieve the same end.

Pershing opened up with artillery and posted his sharpshooters to keep the Moros down as his troops edged closer to the main *cotta*. Along the way, the Americans discovered four abandoned *cottas* and burned them. By nightfall, Pershing was on three sides of the main cotta, careful to leave one side open for the Moros to escape, if they desired. When asked by a reporter if he planned a night assault, Pershing replied, "No. We would lose too many men." The reporter insisted and asked if Pershing was afraid the Moros would escape in the darkness. Pershing told him, "That is exactly what I expect them to do."[3]

At about 3:00 A.M., a group of Moros rushed the American position, but massed rifle fire cut them down before they made much progress. Pershing knew the other Moros were using the diversion to escape. In the morning, Pershing's men found the main *cotta* deserted except for the sultan himself, who immediately charged with his long blade. His honor demanded no less, but honor is poor protection against a battalion of riflemen. Meanwhile, Pershing's burning of the Maciu *cotta* had an immediate effect, bringing him many new Moro friends as they were shocked to see their impregnable fortress reduced to ashes. Moreover, in the immediate aftermath of the assault, Moro attacks on Americans fell away to almost zero.

Next up were the troublesome Moros at Bayan. The Moros in this district were led by an imam, Sajiduciman, who told his followers that since the Americans ate pork and practiced a different religion, any Moros who lived near them or befriended them would go to hell. During 1902, Sajiduciman took advantage of Pershing's inaction to increase the strength of his *cotta,* while also providing materiel support for any Moros who wanted to attack Camp Vickers.

Pershing initially sent him friendly notes, which were ignored. Then, in early December, Pershing sent a final note to Sajiduciman asking him to come make peace or he would make war. A month later, Pershing was invited to visit Sajiduciman at Bayan. He was not so foolish as to go alone this time, and brought with him a strong combined arms force, including artillery. Along the way he saw hundreds of Moros heading for Bayan dressed in their best clothes, something they did for celebrations or when preparing to die. Something was up, but Pershing could not figure out what.

When he arrived at Bayan it became clear. Sajiduciman met with him and then took him on a tour of his fortifications. Pershing in turn turned out his troops to present arms and fired an artillery salvo out into the lake, as both a salute and demonstration of power. These pleasantries out of the way, Sajiduciman brought Pershing over to a group of Moro notables squatting around an ancient copy of the Koran. A delighted Sajiduciman then informed Pershing that the assembled *dattos* had voted to make him a *datto* also. For the first and only time an American became a chief in the Moro nation. Pershing was thunderstruck, but managed to give a short speech on peace and friendship. Before he left, all of the assembled *dattos* swore on the Koran that they would always be friends of the Americans. It was not uncommon thereafter to find Moro infants named for the great *datto* chief, Pershing.

That left only Bacoclod, the strongest fortress in the Lake Lanao region, unpacified. Again, notes of friendship were sent, asking for peace. A single message came back: "What we want is war as we do not desire your friendship. If you come to Bacoclod our priests will circumcise you and your soldiers."

Pershing was convinced that most of the Moros at Bacoclod were simply posturing and that after a few months the main fighting force would melt away to take advantage of what the Americans were offering. But by March 1903, Pershing had to face facts. Attacks by Bacoclod Moros were increasing, and Pershing noted that once again his prestige among other Moros was falling. He asked Sumner's permission to eliminate the Bacoclod *cotta*.

On April 5, Pershing started out. The first day's march was uneventful, but early the next morning he came under fire from a hastily constructed *cotta* manned by Bacoclod allies, the Linok

Moros. Pershing's Moro allies told him the Linoks might resist, but Pershing saw them as a mere diversion and ordered his troops to fire only one volley before marching past them. He later learned that this act broke the Linok will to resist, as it had been a terrible blow to tribal pride to discover that the great Pershing did not consider them worth pausing for a real fight. The Linok Moros melted away in shame.

Arriving at Bacoclod, Pershing implemented the system that had worked so well in the past. After some hard marching in a downpour and through dense jungle, Pershing moved into a position where his artillery and rifles could dominate the massive *cotta*. Firing began immediately and lasted until dark. Once again, Pershing left an escape route open and some of the Moros took advantage of it in the night. The next morning there was a white flag on the *cotta* and the head *datto* emerged to discuss terms. Pershing found his offer to surrender the fort only if his men could keep their weapons unacceptable. The *datto* returned to the *cotta*, hoisted the red flag of war, and the shooting recommenced. By late afternoon, Pershing's artillery had reduced the fort to rubble, while his infantry had edged up close enough to make the final assault.

Pershing, hoping the Moros would either surrender or run away, decided to wait until dawn before attacking. He offered the *datto* a chance to surrender, but the reply clearly demonstrated the cultural divide between the two sides: "If the Americans want to fight us, let them fight. But tell them to fight like men. While my fort is besieged, I see American soldiers down by the waterside eating my coconuts. This is infamous and is not war."

The next day Pershing gave him the war he wanted.

> Under cover of fire from our lines the assaulting troops dashed over the ditch along an improvised bridge and onto the parapet. The remaining effective defenders rushed to the walls to meet the attack. For a few minutes the fighting was hand-to-hand, compilan and kris against

rifle and bayonet. Three of our men were wounded but the others made short work of the opposition. The Moros had made a gallant stand, but were no match in skill or arms for our troops.

Bacolod was taken at a cost of only three American casualties. Sixty Moros were dead in and around the *cotta* and other Moros reported at least another sixty had died of wounds in the jungle. Pershing knew he had broken the back of Moro resistance in the area and stated in his official report: "Destruction of the *cotta* at Bacolod plus Moro losses destroyed their prestige forever and will have a salutary and lasting effect on them."

The expedition's surgeon later gave his vivid impression of Pershing's fighting and command style:

> Had Pershing assaulted on the first or second day, the casualties would have been terrible on our side. By pounding the cotta with artillery and giving its people a chance to escape, he so intimidated the Moros, that when he finally assaulted there only remained in the fort the really desperate characters who were determined to die fighting. . . . [H]ow much different would have been the result had he listened to the impetuous advice of his officers.[4]

Upon his arrival back at Camp Vickers the garrison commander requested that Pershing keep the expeditionary force outside the camp as there was a good chance they had been exposed to cholera along their march route. Exposing the Vickers garrison to even the possibility of cholera would be foolish, but his troops were exhausted and deserved to rest in the relatively comfortable camp. Pershing mulled it over for a moment and then ordered the garrison moved out of Camp Vickers to live in tents, while his expeditionary force took over the camp, proving once again that he both knew how to preserve the lives of his soldiers and that their needs were always uppermost in his thoughts.

+≈≈≈+

There was one final demonstration of American power Pershing wanted to make in order to prove to one and all that Moro resistance was both broken and futile. He decided to march his force around the entire Lake Lanao, something the Spanish had tried several times without success. The march began on May 2, 1903, and took almost two weeks. The troops encountered only half-hearted resistance at two points, which was rapidly dealt with. Along most of the route, however, Pershing met nothing but white flags and cheerful welcomes. One *datto,* whose people had not had much contact with the Americans, sat on the wall of his *cotta* deciding whether to resist. After counting the number of soldiers passing by, he opted for a feast instead. On May 10, Pershing's exhausted command marched back into Vickers—mission accomplished. The march made such an impression on the Moros that American GIs in the Philippines during World War II discovered that many of them used it as the basis of their dating system. For instance, when asked how old he was, a Moro would usually say something to the effect of, "I was born four years after the great Pershing marched around the lake."

Soon after the march's completion, Pershing received orders to return to the United States. He was coming home both as a hero and a celebrity. The march around the lake had captured the imagination of the American people, as had his successful combat actions at Maciu and Bacolod. He had not pacified every Moro on Mindanao, but he had won over the regions assigned to him and had made more progress, with less loss of blood, then any other American. Speculation was rife in the newspapers and even among army officers about Pershing being rewarded with a promotion directly from captain to general. General George Davis, now supreme commander in the Philippines, wrote: "When the time comes for the Department to make the selection of general officers for promotion from the grade of captain, I hope that Captain Pershing may be selected for brigadier general. I have frequently brought his merits to the attention of the Department, in routine and in special communications, for gallantry, good judgment, and through efficiency in every branch of the soldier's profession. He is the equal of any and the superior of most."

CHAPTER 4

Love Gained

BY THE TIME PERSHING RETURNED TO THE UNITED STATES in July 1903, the movement to make him a brigadier general had picked up considerable steam and recommendations were flowing into the War Department on a regular basis. Theodore Roosevelt, who had recently ascended to the presidency after the assassination of William McKinley, seemed poised to act, but then hesitated. While he conceded that Pershing deserved great rewards for his accomplishments in the Philippines, a promotion from captain to general in one jump was too much for Roosevelt to swallow. The president may have liked Pershing, and obviously thought highly of his warrior spirit, which he had witnessed at the Battle of San Juan Hill, but Roosevelt liked a number of other soldiers, too, and some of them had also been close to him during the Spanish-American War.

The issue was important enough for Roosevelt to feel compelled to comment on it during his 1903 address to Congress, which was reproduced in every major newspaper in the country: "When a man renders such service as Captain Pershing rendered last spring in the Moro campaign, it ought to be possible to reward him without at once jumping him to the grade of brigadier general." In the end, the seniority system proved too much to overcome and Pershing's promotion to general was quashed. Roosevelt would have made him a colonel, but the law did not allow for that.

But Pershing had a new interest to take his mind off any disappointment. The forty-three-year-old soldier had fallen in love, apparently for the first time. Her name was Helen Frances Warren and she was the twenty-two-year-old daughter of Senator Francis E. Warren, who was also a cattle baron, the richest man in Wyoming, and the chairman of the Military Affairs Committee. Frances, as she was commonly called, was also wealthy in her own right and owned several properties that earned her $10,000 a year, a prodigious sum in 1903. She was well-educated, quick to laugh, attractive, if not beautiful, and had the kind of charming wit and gaiety that made people want to be around her.

Upon his return to the United States, Pershing was assigned to the army staff in Washington and found that his celebrity brought with it numerous invitations to join the capital's social scene. He later complained that only by sternly refusing most of them was he able to get any work done. Still, because he enjoyed dancing and remained fond of the society of women, the weekly dance at Fort Myer became a regular activity. There, on December 9, 1903, he met Miss Warren. If love at first sight is possible, this was it. Her diary for that day reads: "Went to a hop at Fort Myer. Perfectly lovely time. Met Mr. Pershing, of Moros and Presidential message fame." By December 11, she was writing, "I have lost my heart"; and on the eighteenth she wrote, " . . . have lost my heart to Capt. Pershing irretrievably."

For his part, Pershing was just as love struck. On the night he met Miss Warren he broke into a friend's room, woke him from a sound sleep, and announced, "I've met the girl God made for me." Then he proceeded to ask his friend what he thought on the big issues. Should an old man like him consider being with such a young girl? Could a captain afford to support a lady who grew up rich? Would she be the kind of woman that could put up with army life? What his friend thought was that Pershing should leave him alone, "John, maybe you're in love and can do without sleep. But I'm not."[1]

They may have told close personal friends they were in love, but it was many months before they got around to telling each other. When Pershing was transferred to the Midwest for a new duty assignment, they wrote each other several times a day, but their letters demonstrated a stark formality beyond even the custom of the day. It was not until late April that he wrote that he loved her, but still signed the letter John J. Pershing. And it was not until the following summer that they began to use first names in addressing each other in letters. The corner turned when Pershing went to stay with Frances and her family on their ranch in Wyoming, and Pershing first kissed her. Later he wrote of that kiss, "I never kissed your lips until we both said we loved each other. I should not have done so under any other circumstances. That kiss, as all others have been, was attended with feelings that to me are divinely sacred."[2] It was all very quaint and also very un-Pershing. He was forty-three years old and had been known for decades as a ladies' man. However, something in Frances Warren brought out a tender side that Pershing had not revealed to any previous paramour.

By the time the couple came back to Washington, everyone assumed they would be married. It was just a matter of setting the date. They became engaged on Christmas Day 1904, with plans to marry the following June. Pershing had just received new orders assigning him to the American Embassy in Japan as the military attaché and he was to report as soon as possible. The ambassador had requested, and the army staff had agreed to send, a bachelor familiar with the game of bridge. Pershing went to secretary of war William Howard Taft, and explained that he barely knew the game of bridge and was engaged to be married. After laughing uproariously, Taft asked Pershing if he were a bachelor as of that moment. Pershing confirmed he was, whereupon Taft asked if had already received orders sending him to Japan. Again, Pershing confirmed he had. The answer was simple, explained Taft—accept the orders and then get married. No one was going to revoke orders because a soldier had gotten himself married, and the army did not assign officers based on their ability to play cards.

Pershing had sought the assignment to Japan, as the Russo-Japanese War was raging, and he was eager to visit the front as an observer. His wedding was moved up to January 26, barely a month after the engagement, and though the couple originally planned a small wedding, they ended up sending out over 4,500 invitations. The event took place in the teeth of a blizzard, which did not, however, stop most of official Washington from attending, including the president and most of Congress, which had adjourned for the day so members could attend the ceremony. The usually aloof Pershing wrote later to Frances, "I am the happiest man in the world and have the dearest, loveliest wife" and "millions of kisses from the craziest lover that ever wrote a line to his sweetheart. . . . Wife and sweetheart in one, and all mine."[3]

The Pershings enjoyed a short honeymoon in Wyoming before sailing for Japan. While in Wyoming, Pershing saved an eight-year-old girl who was being dragged along a hard road by her horse. After checking that she had only suffered a few bruises, he insisted she remount immediately. The girl resisted and cried, but Pershing picked her up, sat her on the horse, and forced her to ride it all the way back to her home as he followed. He explained in words she would always remember, "If I had not made you ride home you might always be nervous about horses. . . . Now for a word of advice and don't forget this. If you have a fall—mental, moral, or physical—pick yourself up and start over again immediately. If you do, in the long run life won't beat you."[4]

⊹══⊰⊱══⊹

Husband and wife arrived in Japan on March 5, 1905, and four days later Pershing headed for the front with Russia. By the time Pershing arrived, the great battles for Mukden and Port Arthur were over, but the Russian army, though defeated, was still in the field, and there was a lot of hard fighting left to be done. The Russo-Japanese War was the only major conflict between 1870 and 1914, and every nation sent observers to watch developments and record the lessons. Just as the later Spanish Civil War would be used by European powers to experiment with new technologies and doctrine, many world powers were keen to discover how the awesome technological achievements since 1870 had changed the nature of war.

At first Pershing, like most other observers, was stymied in his efforts to get to the battle front. One Japanese officer explained his country's lack of accommodation by saying that the lessons Western officers were looking to learn were being paid for with Japanese blood. Desperate to get to the front, Pershing wrote a letter to his adjutant general in Washington, saying that if he was not going to be allowed to see anything, he might as well be posted elsewhere. As Pershing expected, the censor noted the remark and reported it to his superiors. Always sensitive to criticism, the local commanders made it a point to get Pershing to the front.

Pershing spent several months observing the war and walked away with new impressions of how future wars would be fought and what the cost would be. He was now convinced that modern wars, fought by industrial powers, made brilliant maneuvers almost irrelevant to victory—something that had still been possible as late as the Franco-Prussian War of 1870–71. In the future there would be no war-ending decisive victories such as Austerlitz. The Russians had lost great battles at Mukden and Port Arthur and the Japanese had paid for both cites with casualties in the hundreds of thousands. But they were still confronted by a large Russian army with plenty of fight left in it. Pershing became convinced that the Japanese army was fought out, and later came to see that Japan won the war in the Washington peace negotiations, not on the battlefield. For the first time, Pershing was seeing the face of modern war, and the lessons stayed with him.

Gone were the days when the army commander could personally direct the deployment of his troops. When Napoleon had won his great victory at Austerlitz, he stood on the Pratzen Heights and surveyed the entire battlefield. This was now impossible, as modern armies were already five or ten times the size either side had possessed at Austerlitz, and were spread out over dozens, and even hundreds, of miles. In the future, wars would not be won by heroic leaders, but by men who could handle the problems of administration.

Foremost among these required administrative skills was the ability to master the supply system. Pershing took careful note of the huge expenditures of artillery ammunition required to dominate the modern battlefield and the vast amounts of other materiel needed to maintain hundreds of thousands of men in the field for a sustained campaign. Bravery, tactical flexibility, and the warrior instinct still counted in battle, but they all faded to insignificance when compared to the importance of creating an effective controlling organization led by a master technocrat.

Pershing filed his lessons with the War Department and in his own mind, and returned to Japan in September 1906. His arrival coincided with two happy events, the birth of his first child (Helen), and twelve days later his promotion to brigadier general. Roosevelt had promoted him over 257 captains, 364 majors, 131 lieutenant colonels, and 110 colonels—a total of 862 more senior officers. Public and institutional reaction to the promotion was swift and mostly negative. Promoting an officer to general so quickly after his marriage to the daughter of a powerful senator led to conspiracy theories and the press openly speculated that Senator Warren had told the president that his pet legislation would have an easier time in the Congress if his son-in-law were to become a general. Others said this was a payoff for Pershing's leading his Tenth Cavalry troopers to Roosevelt's rescue at San Juan Hill and then letting the all-white Rough Riders take the lion's share of the credit, which rocketed Roosevelt's political career forward.

Forgotten in the media storm was Pershing's incredible performance in the Philippines, the fact that every general in the army had recommended the promotion and that such a promotion was not unprecedented. In fact, three generals serving when Pershing was made a general had been promoted directly from captain to general officer: Albert L. Mills, Leonard Wood, and J. Franklin Bell—the last over 1,031 seniors.[5] It would be hard to deny that having Senator Warren as a father-in-law contributed to the decision, and later in life Pershing admitted as much. However, it probably was only the difference of the promotion coming in 1906 rather than a year or two later. No one doubted that Pershing deserved the promotion, but the resulting uproar was strong enough for the president to finally publish a letter he had sent to Senator Warren: "The promotion was made solely on the merits, and unless I am mistaken you never spoke to me on the subject until I announced that he had been promoted. To promote a man because he marries a senator's daughter would be an infamy; and to refuse him promotion for the same reason would be an equal infamy."

Like most political tempests, this one quickly subsided and the Senate unanimously approved the promotion. But hard on the heels of Pershing's promotion came a scandal that almost destroyed everything. He was charged in the press with having maintained a Filipino mistress while serving in the Moro district, and of having sired two children with her. In the United States, which has always had a strong streak of puritan morality, this was the kind of sensation that could shatter a military career.

Pershing recognized the danger and moved rapidly to quell the rumor. He not only made public denials, but also sent personal letters to his friends and others with influence refuting the charges. Pershing collected sworn affidavits from those who knew him in the Philippines and even from the lady in question and her husband, all of them maintaining Pershing's innocence. Still, the bulk of the media, always ready to run with a good sex scandal, continued to print the scandalous stories from an anonymous source. That source insisted that three other officers knew about Pershing's mistress, and he named names. One of these so-called witnesses was dead and the other two issued public denials. One of them, Captain Thomas Swobe, wrote:

> For two years I was in constant daily almost hourly contact with Pershing at Zamboanga Mindanao. We messed at the same table, our rooms were in the same building and very close to each other. We walked together, rode together—drank from the same bottle, and I know Pershing as any man living knows him. And no more honorable upright, manly and soldierly man than Pershing ever wore soldier straps. And I am ready to defend him against any charge his enemies may bring, and if necessary am ready and willing to go to Washington and appear before the Senate committee for that purpose.

In time, the preponderance of evidence clearing Pershing of the charges shifted the tide, even in the media, which began publishing articles about the factor that jealousy of passed-over officers played in the baseless charges. Through it all, Frances stood by him. Despite published rumors that she was considering divorce, the idea never entered her mind. When she first heard about the charges, Pershing was away, and she immediately wrote to him:

"You know that my love is the same whether it [the rumor] is true or not. If they are able to substantiate the charges, I would love you more than ever because your need of me would be greater." Moral support was what Pershing needed from her most, but Frances went a step further and wrote a short note to her father to dictate the law: "You stand by Jack, no matter what infamy may be said of him." The family closed ranks and it was enough.[6]

+>==≡<+

Pershing left Japan in January 1907 for Fort McKinley in the Philippines, where he commanded for twenty months. Here, he was in charge of a full brigade of troops, which, at the time, was the largest concentration of American forces outside the United States. He was utterly amazed at how few officers understood their responsibilities when it came to conducting extended military operations—as the brigade was focused on its garrison duties and neglecting training for war. Pershing remedied this by instituting a series of maneuvers that paid particular attention to the problems of combined cavalry, infantry, and artillery operations in coordination with one another.

During one of these training exercises, Pershing revealed what was to be a characteristic trait of his leadership. He had ordered an engineer lieutenant to build a bridge over a river swollen with rain. After a while the lieutenant returned and informed Pershing that the bridge could not be built as the river was too high, and he could not get the first rope across. "I never ask the impossible of any officer or soldier in my command," Pershing replied. "When you get an order you must find a way to execute it. Now come with me." Pershing rode rapidly to the river, fastened a rope to his own saddle and crossed the river on horseback. Soon after, the bridge was under construction.[7]

A brigade was a miniscule formation compared to what Pershing would build in 1917, but it was here that he taught himself, and many others, the basic requirements his profession would demand of them in the Great War. He became so enamored with the training opportunities available at Fort McKinley that he wrote General Leonard Wood, then commander of the army in the Philippines, and recommended that he rotate other brigades through the post on a regular basis for intensive operational training, exactly like the army now does at its National Training Center in the deserts of California. Wood turned down the suggestion, claiming that deployments must be governed by the military requirements of the time and that it would involve too great a hardship. Wood failed to foresee the military challenges the country would face in the coming years. A cadre of officers who had gone through Pershing's training regimen would have been invaluable in the Great War, less then a decade away. Tens of thousands of American doughboys paid the ultimate sacrifice for the neglect of training in favor of expediency.

It was at Fort McKinley where Pershing acclimated himself to the demands and even the idea that he was a general officer. At first he was noticeably awkward in his dealings with the large number of majors and colonels at the post. After all, only weeks before they had been senior to him in rank, and they were now expected to defer to him as their commander. He did, however, develop a good relationship with the enlisted men, whose care was always at the top of his list of concerns.

Fort McKinley was also the showcase outpost of the new American empire and as such it attracted a number of VIP guests. Among the more distinguished was the current secretary of war and future president, William Howard Taft. His visit required a formal dinner and Taft was a bit chagrined to find he had not brought a waistcoat with him. Moreover, none could be found on post capable of enclosing his considerable girth in cloth. In the end, Pershing borrowed a waistcoat and cut it along the back seam so it could be pinned to the front of Taft's shirt.

Despite his 325-pound frame and relative immobility, Taft insisted on touring deep into the interior of the country. The trip, by horse, was twenty-five miles in each direction and an absolutely miserable experience for Taft. He wrote to General Wood complaining of the heat, his soreness, and detailed a host of other physical complaints. Wood sent back a one-sentence note to Pershing: "How is the poor damn horse?"

Wood was not the only wit in the Philippines. Pershing's immediate boss was General John Weston, commander of the department of Luzon, whose personality and humor endeared him to Pershing. In one conversation discussing the exploits of the arctic explorer Major General Adolphus Greeley, some of those present commented on how terrible it must have been that during Greeley's last expedition the men were so starved that they were forced to eat the flesh of their dead. Weston, who knew Greely, was then asked what command the army should next offer to the unfortunate explorer. To which he replied, "Hard to tell about poor Greely, why he only ever had but the one small command and he ate it."

All too soon, Pershing was ordered back to Washington. Because his health had deteriorated somewhat in the heat of the Philippines, he decided to take some of his leave time and head home by way of the cool climates of Czarist Russia and then across Europe. His unpublished autobiography has page after page of his remembrances of the trip and for the most part they read as exactly what the trip was—a long family vacation. As far as his future was concerned, the only really relevant item was his observations of Germany. He found the country to have the most regimented society he ever encountered and considered this trait would make them a formidable opponent in the event of war. This impression was further solidified when he visited a local German army headquarters and witness some small-scale maneuvers. After being briefed on German mobilization plans, he remarked, "I have never before seen such perfect preparation."[8]

Pershing eventually arrived back in the United States and took up residence in the Willard Hotel, where his father-in-law also lived. While in Washington, he took part in Howard Taft's inaugural ball and said his official farewells to outgoing President Teddy Roosevelt. His heart, however, was back in the Philippines, and he openly craved a return there to become governor of the Moro Province. Unbeknownst to him, the orders had already been cut to for him to assume that position. But before he could depart, Pershing's heart palpitations and general health worsened. There were even rumors that ill health would force his early retirement. He had consulted a German specialist about his heart while traveling through Europe and was given a less then encouraging prognosis.

Somewhat apprehensive, Pershing checked into the Army and Navy Hospital in Arkansas, where the doctor in charge was a former West Point classmate of Pershing. After several days of tests, Pershing told his old friend to give him the news. The doctor's diagnosis shocked Pershing: "John we have subjected you to every known test, and in my opinion and that of my associates there isn't a damn thing the matter with you." Pershing resisted this opinion, as by now he was convinced there was something seriously wrong with him. When the doctor ordered him to go riding the next day, he did so with some trepidation and told the other doctors he did not expect to survive the trip. But he did survive and after two weeks of rest and exercise he considered himself fit to return to the Philippines.

CHAPTER 5

Victory Gained and Love Lost

PERSHING RETURNED TO THE PHILIPPINES ON NOVEMBER 11, 1909, and would remain there as military governor of the Moro Province until 1913. The Moro Province included two main islands—Mindanao and Jolo—and hundreds of smaller ones. It was divided into five districts, one of which was Pershing's first command on his first tour in the Philippines, the Lanao Lake District. The population of the two islands was over 520,000, of which 325,000 were Moros and 85,000 were Filipinos. The rest consisted of a number of wild inland tribes. Pershing was both civil governor and military commander of the province, and he kept two separate offices located in different buildings. He usually spent mornings in one and afternoons in the other.

Pershing was not happy with his new command and was greatly disappointed to find that much of his progress in befriending the Moros during his last tour in the region had been undone in the intervening years. As Pershing saw it, the main problem was that there was a bewildering number of ethnic groups and cultures in the province, none of which got along with the others. Much like the early American presence in Iraq, rather then try and understand these individual cultures and work with them to bring stability to the island, the Americans had mostly retreated to large fortified bases in the Phillipines. When they did interact with the locals it was mostly in the form of brutal reprisals for native attacks or insults.

Pershing wrote about the ethnic mixture and the ensuing problems this mixture caused: "It was a strange conglomeration of people. Bringing them thoroughly under control, to terminate warfare among them and lead them to a better way of life was an undertaking never seriously attempted. The work required careful judgment and continual patience as well as force and the willingness to use it."

Pershing also had to pacify large numbers of Moros, who had become increasingly alienated from the local government and hostile to Americans. In doing this he had the grudging support of the senior commander in the Philippines, General Leonard Wood, and the unstinting support of the governor general, Cameron Forbes. Pershing's relations with Wood were always strained, possibly as a result of Pershing speaking out about Wood's proposal to retreat at San Juan Hill in 1898, but his relations with Forbes were excellent. The two men shared many common interests and often found that the best way to discuss problems was while hunting together.

While on a trip with Pershing and Forbes to discuss matters, local tribesmen were reluctant to accept a Pershing-Forbes solution to a boundary dispute with an adjacent tribe. To avoid bloodshed, the tribe agreed to decide the issue with a baseball game against the Americans. According to Pershing, "The Governor General covered one base, the Secretary of the Interior another and I the last. Aides and secretaries took other positions in the nine. The natives, although new at the game, played well and were surprised that they did not win, as they had been practicing." Defeated in baseball, the tribe honorably accepted the peace arrangement.

＋＞＝＝＜＋

Most problems proved more intractable and Pershing was worried by what had transpired in the six years since he left Camp Vicars. He judged that military force had often been used unnecessarily and counterproductively: "Though force has to be used to a certain extent, and to the utmost limits when dealing with criminal elements, it was clear that there had been too much haste in using arms to enforce laws and regulations that ran counter to age-old customs." Pershing knew that much more could be gained with patience and appeals to good judgment, and he was particularly disturbed to discover that "in the Lanao District, where I had so many good friends among the Moros, the chiefs had been alienated."

To assess the extent of the problems, Pershing went on a listening tour of the province. At each stop he gathered the chiefs and other headmen, most of whom knew of Pershing or remembered him, and patiently listened to all of their complaints: "I encouraged them to speak frankly and most of them did." Although the meetings were serious in character, they were always colorful, sometimes amusing. At Jolo, the weak and repulsive Sultan's greatest complaint was about the infidelity of his two youngest wives. When Pershing got to Lanao he was greeted as a returned hero. The lead Sultan approached him and said, "Since you left we have been like orphans, with no hope except in God, but now that you are returning we are very happy and glad."

Pershing immediately instituted programs that could serve as a model for counterinsurgency planning today. In one of his first acts, he broke up the concentrations of troops and distributed them in small pockets throughout the province. The mere presence of well-armed soldiers in every populated locality had an immediate stabilizing effect, which in turn led to rapid economic growth.

He also gave these soldiers a guiding principle: Ensure that Moro feelings and dignity are always respected to the utmost levels possible. When Pershing himself dealt with the Moros, he began almost every meeting with some version of the following statement: "I wish to impress upon the Moros here that this is the country of the Moros; that they are the strongest race that I have seen on the island. Again I wish to state that this is not the country of the Americans, but this is the country of the Moros, and we are not going to bring Americans here to push you out."[1]

During his time as governor, Pershing constructed 200 miles of telephone lines, 500 miles of roads, and thirty-seven medical stations for Moro and tribal use. The Moros greatly appreciated the roads, and considered them the finest thing they had ever seen. He also reformed the law codes and put most of the decision-making authority back in the local courts, where Moros could be judged by other Moros and not by Americans or by the hated Filipinos. Pershing also spent about one-sixth of province revenue on education, although the hatred Moros felt for Filipinos hindered his efforts, as most teachers were Filipinos, whom the Moros considered only fit for slavery.

All of these actions worked to revitalize the province's economy, which was Pershing's preeminent concern. He established new trading stations throughout the province for Moros to sell their own goods and undertook to make sure everything the Moros required to become economically productive was available from the government at a reasonable cost. Pershing also ran trading fairs, the largest of which was held at Zamboanga in February 1911. Pershing used this fair not only to bring all the Moros and various tribes into contact with one another, but also to demonstrate the awesome power and benefits of Western civilization. Two items in particular impressed the Moros: the great battleship anchored in the harbor and the merry-go-round.

Slowly, and with infinite patience, Pershing brought peace, stability, and prosperity to the province. Unfortunately, two major problems persisted. The first was the Filipino local government's constant attempts to extend their authority into Moro-dominated areas. Pershing knew that the mere attempt of Filipinos to rule over the Moros would jeopardize all of his achievements. The Moros viewed the Filipinos' repeated demands for independence from the United States as veiled attempts to get the Americans out of the way and allow Filipino extermination of them.

This point was brought home to Pershing during one of his larger tribal meetings, at which the governor General Forbes was in attendance, when an old Moro sultan stood to speak after listening to Filipino speeches calling for independence: "We want American rule and ask the government not be turned over to the Filipinos. I am an old man and hoped to see no more fighting, but if the Americans leave we will not submit to the Filipinos, but I will lead my people again into battle." While Pershing was in command, he resisted all attempts by the Filipinos to extend their influence to the province. Given the current state of affairs between Mindanao (where there is an ongoing Islamic insurgency) and the Filipino central government today, one might wonder if both sides would have been better served if Pershing had worked harder to develop a political compromise between the two parties.

The other major problem was bandits and other outlaws, a category in which Pershing also lumped the *juramentado* terrorists. To combat the outlaws, Pershing dispatched flying columns on a regular basis to pursue and exterminate bandit groups. This program had some success and the troops boasted a considerable bandit body count from year to year. However, as soon as one bandit group was dealt final justice, another would emerge to replace it. As Pershing later wrote: "It was the Moro outlaws who kept the province in a constant state of turmoil and there was hardly a day after my arrival that a report did not come in of some outrage somewhere in the province."

However it was the *juramentados,* as distinct from the bandits, that caused his biggest consternation. While the bandits normally confined their activities to rural areas, the *juramentados* would often strike in the centers of large towns, which Pershing viewed as a direct assault on civilization itself. Pershing advocated the adoption of any measure that might stem this relatively constant stream of terrorist enlistees. One tactic which did prove somewhat effective has become a hot topic of internet rumor and debate since 9/11. Did Pershing advocate burying dead *juramentados* in pigskins or with pigs? Until now the historical verdict was that this is a vicious rumor, and while it may have happened on occasion, Pershing neither knew about it nor, given his humane outlook, would he have condoned such action. That verdict is wrong, as Pershing's own unpublished autobiography states:

> These *juramentado* attacks were materially reduced in number by a practice the army had already adopted, one that the Mohammedans held in abhorrence. The bodies were publicly buried in the same grave with a dead pig. It was not pleasant to have to take such measures but the prospect of going to hell instead of heaven sometimes deterred the would-be assassins.

In the early spring of 1911 continued outlaw activities and *juramentado* outbreaks were pushing Pershing toward radical action. He related the incident that pushed him over the edge:

> A particularly cruel case was that of the killing of Lieutenant W. H. Rodney, of the Second Cavalry, one Sunday afternoon in Jolo, close to the barracks. The Lieutenant was out walking with his little daughter, about five years old, when a Moro who passed him on the road suddenly drew his barong, turned and killed him with several quick and vicious slashes from behind. . . . He was after Americans and going about his purpose he calmly proceeded towards the barracks. But the commanding officer had seen

the attack and called out the guard, who shot the man dead in his tracks.

To put an end to this and other attacks, Pershing decided to disarm the entire Moro population. He realized that this was not something the Moros would easily accept, as their hand-crafted weapons were handed down generation to generation and revered as sacred items. From Pershing's viewpoint, however, disarming the Moros and pagan tribes was the only way to guarantee peaceful civilian rule. While many American officials, including General Wood, thought it an impossible and absurd task, Pershing received Forbes's full support.

On September 8, 1911, Pershing issued a proclamation making it illegal for anyone in the province to possess firearms or to carry cutting and thrusting weapons. People were given until December 1 to turn in their weapons and receive fair compensation. After that deadline, Pershing intended to take them away by force. As he expected, those peaceably inclined and his old friends were soon lining up to turn in their weapons, but hostile elements immediately began to group themselves for action. Word was sent to Pershing that, if he wanted their weapons, he would have to come and take them and be prepared to pay a high price in blood.

Though there was some resistance to the proclamation in all of the province's five districts, the hotbeds were centered in Jolo and Lanao. According to Pershing, "For years the good people of these areas had been harassed by outlaw bands whose disarmament could be accomplished only by the energetic use of force." When Moros rushed an American camp in Jolo, killing one and wounding three, Pershing decided that time for action had arrived and left for Jolo to take charge personally.

Pershing divided his forces into two field commands, one of which was at Taglibi, eight miles west of the walled town of Jolo. It was here that Pershing expected the worst trouble. He had his men dig entrenchments, clear the jungle for 200 yards in every direction, and lay copious amounts of barbed wire. On the night of November 28, the Moros attacked. They came on recklessly and threw themselves on the barbed wire in a frenzied series of attempts to come to close quarters with the Americans. But for the wire, the fighting would have been hand-to-hand. As it was, each assault was broken by disciplined rifle fire and by dawn the field was littered with Moro dead. The American force suffered no losses.

Still, attacks persisted on any American leaving the camps and by December 2, Pershing decided to send out flying columns to punish the recalcitrant Moros. A note he sent to his wife reflects his thinking at the time:

> I would give anything to end this business without much fighting, but the Taglibi Moros seem vicious. They have shown their teeth and snapped at us. But you can't talk a fellow around to much of anything if he is shooting at you all the time. I have always said that it is an error to sit idly by and let these savages shoot at you without going after them, politics or no politics, and I do not intend to permit it.

Two days later, five flying columns marched into the Taglibi region from different directions, all converging on the Moro stronghold at Bud Dajo. Pershing had received intelligence that the Moros had concentrated several hundred fighters along with their families and built a well-fortified *cotta* at the location. Four years earlier there had been a battle at Bud Dajo in which the American force had lost eighteen men and fifty-two had been wounded. However, the Moros had lost over 600 people, men, women, and children. The striking disparity in the losses and the fact that so many children were killed led to front-page stories in the United States about "wanton slaughter" inflicted on innocents. The Senate had even been pressed to pass several resolutions condemning army actions.

In keeping with his past practice, Pershing gave the Moros every chance to surrender or escape into the jungle. Reports were reaching him, however, that the Moros at Bud Dajo had all taken an oath to fight to the death. Discouraged by their obstinacy, Pershing sent another note to his wife, as his men encircled the fortified *cotta:* "I am sorry the Moros are such fools—but this Dojo will not mean the slaughter of woman and children, nor hasty assaults against strong attachments. I shall lose as few men and kill as few Moros as possible."

Taking a lesson from medieval siege operations, Pershing invested the Moro *cotta* with strong positions along each of seventeen trails he found leading up to it, with outposts stretched along the spaces between these fortified positions. Each day, Pershing moved his positions closer to the *cotta,* building five separate lines of investment, until he was within thirty yards of the Moro position. Escape was now impossible, although the Moros persisted in trying to break through. Each attempt was repulsed by heavy rifle fire, until the almost starving Moros began to give up the fight. At first, they deserted in small groups, but after a few days they began approaching Pershing's lines in groups of 50 to 200. By Christmas Eve the *cotta* was empty, but there were some Moros unaccounted for. Pershing knew they were lurking in the jungle, hoping the Americans would go away now that the *cotta* was deserted. Pershing put every soldier he had in line and settled down to wait. That night, the remaining Moros launched one last fierce attack, which was predictably shattered by rifle volleys delivered at close range. In the morning, forty-nine survivors surrendered and the *cotta* was destroyed. Pershing's greatest satisfaction, however, was that it was all accomplished without undo spilling of innocent blood, as no women and children had been killed. He was further pleased upon receiving a note from Forbes calling his conduct of the battle masterful.

Within six months of this operation, the Americans had collected practically all Moro firearms with the exception of one group led by the Datto Amil. Pershing considered this group the most "stubborn, defiant, and difficult" in the province and despaired of disarming them through reason or financial incentive. As usual, the Moros had built a powerful *cotta*, this time at Bud Bagsak, and populated it with women and children along with their warriors. Once again, Pershing hoped to avoid a general slaughter and allowed negotiations to drag on for months. Finally, Pershing agreed to remove his troops from the district in return for the Moros handing over their weapons. Pershing withdrew, but the Moros failed to uphold their end of the bargain, though a large number of them left the *cotta* to return to their farms. Pershing continued to negotiate, as he secretly prepared for a lightning attack on Bud Bagsak while the women and children were at their farms.

On June 11, in total secrecy, Pershing collected his troops from various locations and by both land march and amphibious landing moved rapidly on the *cotta* complex around Bud Bagsak. The assault was so rapid that it was impossible for the Moros to recall their families into the *cotta* complex. Pershing had achieved his first objective: There would be no massacre of women and children, but he still faced hundreds of desperate Moro warriors prepared to fight to the death in defense of their "impregnable" *cottas*.

Pershing's rapid advance caught the first line of defenders napping and their *cottas* quickly fell to a surprise assault with no American losses. Seizing the advantage, Pershing ordered his columns forward through some of the harshest terrain in the Philippines. Often his troops, unable to find a road or trail, spent hours cutting their way through the jungle. Despite the hardships, Pershing pushed his main body on relentlessly, while detaching Major George Shaw on one of the toughest jobs of the operation: to clear the *cotta* at Pujagan. This was almost as formidable an obstacle as the one at Bud Bagsak. However, Shaw was a man who knew his business and had served under Pershing when he was reducing *cottas* to rubble in 1903, so he had a good idea of the Pershing method.

Shaw's men cut their way to a position where they could dominate the *cotta,* and then called for its surrender. When his request was predictably refused, he began pounding the *cotta* with his field cannons, which he kept well out of range of the Moro guns. While the *cotta* was being reduced by artillery, Shaw had his men dig entrenchments in a circle to await the anticipated Moro assault. Before dark, he moved the field guns into the center of the perimeter, assembled deadly canister rounds, and had the fuses cut to zero. In effect, he had turned his cannons into super-powerful shotguns.

Throughout the night, the Moros beat drums, shouted insults, and built up their courage. In the morning they could be seen dressed in their most colorful finery and old-timers in Shaw's trenches told the recruits to prepare because the Moros were dressed to die and would be coming soon. At 9:30 A.M. they poured out of the *cotta* and headed straight for Shaw's position. The Moros came on waving their barongs and krises, shouting blood-curdling screams and throwing spears. Shaw's veterans decimated them with heavy disciplined fire, until they disappeared in a fold in the ground. Then, screaming like banshees, they suddenly reappeared only fifty feet from Shaw's positions. Shaw's men stood in their trenches firing as fast as they could and at that moment the field guns fired their canister rounds, sweeping the field in front of them and leaving only death in their wake. The Moro assault was not just broken; it was annihilated.

While Shaw was defeating the Pujagan *cotta,* the rest of Pershing's forces continued the advance on Bud Bagsak. By June 14, Pershing had managed to get his field guns into position to begin softening up the *cotta* for a final assault the next morning. For this attack Pershing intended to use mainly Philippine scouts, who were mostly Moros serving under American officers. On the morning of June 15, the field guns started early, and at 9:00 A.M. Pershing ordered two companies of scouts to advance. He also directed American officers to trail behind the scouts and direct the fighting from more secure positions to the rear of the fighting line. At first, the mountain guns and supporting small arms fire made the advance easy, but as the scouts entered the *cotta's* trench system the defense became tenacious. In a letter to his wife, Pershing said, "The fighting was the fiercest I have ever seen." This was the last stand of the Moros and they fought like devils.[2]

The fighting went on for nine hours. All of it was at close quarters and much of it was hand-to-hand. The American force had been greatly disappointed by the new hand grenades they had been furnished—specifically their lack of punch. So, for this battle they used sticks of dynamite tied in bundles of four. This proved effective, except for those times when the Moro defenders threw them back. By 1:30 P.M., Pershing's men were within 100 meters of the main *cotta,* but casualties were mounting and the attack was faltering. Pershing moved to the front line, dodging arrows and spears, as he directed the fight. He realized this was the climax of the fight and ordered the American officers to move to the front, in order to stop directing and start leading. Pershing's aide said, "The effect was electric." New energy went into the attack as American officers, ignoring heavy fire occurring all around them, threw themselves at the bamboo fences and began tearing them down. The Philippine scouts poured through the gaps and flanked the Moros in their trenches. The Moros still fought hard, but it was an increasingly futile effort. By 4:30 P.M. the *cotta* was declared secured and the last Moro resistance was crushed.

+≫═•═≪+

Soon after the battle, Pershing was nominated for the Medal of Honor. Upon hearing this, Pershing rushed a note off to the War Department requesting that the award not be granted. "I do not consider that my action on that occasion was such as to entitle me to be decorated with a Medal of Honor. I went to that part of the line because my presence there was needed." The decorations board agreed with Pershing. In 1922, after Congress created the Distinguished Service Cross (DSC), the decorations board again reviewed his actions and recommended he receive this new award. Pershing, who was chief of staff at the time and had veto authority over the board's recommendations, voted down his own award. In 1940, sixteen years after his retirement, President Roosevelt summoned him to the White House and on Pershing's eightieth birthday awarded him the DSC.

Immediately after the fight at Bud Bagsak, Pershing returned to the task of building roads, clinics, and schools. For the rest of his time in the province, Pershing focused on enriching and improving the lives of the Moros and converting the nomadic inland tribes to a life of settled agriculture. His endeavors made remarkable progress until August 1913, when his health began to deteriorate. After being hospitalized for a combination of aliments, Pershing judged his effectiveness as a commander in the Philippines at an end and requested reassignment. In December, the War Department ordered him home to command the Eighth Brigade at the Presidio in San Francisco.

+>——=+

Pershing and his family arrived in San Francisco just after the New Year and settled into new quarters at the Presidio. His health improved rapidly, and he later remembered the few months he spent there with his family as one of the happier periods of his life. His family had now grown, to four children. Since the children had spent most of their youth in the Philippines, everything in America was new and amazing to them. Since his official duties at the Presidio were light compared to the Philippines, Pershing had time to take the children on various outings, including a memorable trip to see Buffalo Bill Cody's Wild West Show, where Pershing discovered, much to his amazement, that a number of the Sioux Indians in the show had ridden with him as scouts during the Ghost Dance Uprising.

This happy family interlude was cut short by trouble brewing on the Mexican border. Rumors were flying about that the Mexican insurgent Pancho Villa was planning to cross the border and raid El Paso. To forestall that attack and secure the area, at the end of April 1914, Pershing and his Eighth Brigade were ordered to El Paso. Upon his arrival, Pershing discovered there was no truth to the rumors, but he was ordered to stay at the border and assume command of the troops in the area, which included Fort Bliss, just outside El Paso. As time dragged on, it seemed that Pershing would remain at Fort Bliss for a prolonged period. He ordered his quarters fixed up and began making arrangements for his family to join him.

Toward the end of August, Frances Pershing sent her husband a letter: "The world is so clean this morning. There is the sound of meadow larks everywhere. And God be thanked for the sunshine and blue sky! Do you think there can be many people in the world as happy as we are? I would like to live to be a thousand years old if I could spend all of that time with you."[3] Before Pershing received the letter, on August 26, 1915, Frances Pershing and her three daughters were killed. Only Pershing's son Warren survived a horrific blaze that ripped through their Presidio home.

Frances had overnight guests when the fire broke out and that family managed to escape. In the dark, those fighting the fire believed only the Pershing family was occupying the house and that it was they who had exited the building. The rescuers were prepared to let the old house burn to the ground when a shout went up that the Pershings were actually still in the home. Despite the raging inferno, a dozen bystanders stormed through the flames and entered the house. The family was pulled out through upstairs windows and although desperate efforts were made to revive them, only Warren responded.[4]

Pershing had been dealt a devastating blow. Friends who saw him at the time said he was crushed. Some worried about his ability to ever recover. When he arrived at the Presidio, Pershing first went to pray over the bodies of his wife and daughters and then to pick up his son at Lettermen Army Hospital. As Pershing and young Warren were driven away from the hospital, they passed the country fairgrounds. Pershing asked Warren if he had been to the fair and the boy replied, "Oh yes, Mommy takes us all the time." On hearing this Pershing began to tremble so badly that he became incapable of holding the boy and had to hand him to another passenger.

Those who knew Pershing well said the tragedy changed him. He had always been a silent and introverted man and in that regard Frances had been good for him. She brought Pershing to life. When she passed away he retreated deeper into himself. While he was still warm and even humorous at times with close friends, it became increasingly difficult for anyone new to break through Pershing's hard outer shell. Despite burying himself in work, the pain of his loss never lessened. Twenty years later, while visiting friends, he was asked why he appeared so sad. He replied, "Today is my daughter's birthday."[5]

CHAPTER 6

Chasing Villa

AT 4:15 A.M., MARCH 9, 1916, PANCHO VILLA LED 425 Mexican insurgents into Columbus, New Mexico. By the end of the raid, his men had killed eighteen American citizens. Talking to a journalist after the event, Villa insulted the American soldiers guarding Columbus by saying, "I was awake; they were asleep, and it took them too long to wake up." In reality, Villa did not just ride in, kill eighteen Americans, and ride out unscathed. While he may have surprised the soldiers, they reacted quickly and blasted Villa's raiding party to pieces. When Villa finally rode out, he left over 200 of his men dead or bleeding in the streets. His raid did, however, have one major effect. It lit the fuse on what was already a delicate situation. Mexican raiders had invaded U.S. territory and killed American citizens. The U.S. public demanded action.

The years that led up to the Columbus raid saw Mexico in a state of crisis. For over thirty years Porfirio Diaz had ruled Mexico with an iron fist, but as he aged, his grip on power slipped until, in 1911, Francisco Madero eventually overthrew him. Madero was a revolutionary thinker but he lacked the hard steel in his gut of a Lenin or Mao. Within months, the commander of the Mexican armed forces, General Victoriano Huerta, overthrew and executed Madero. Newly elected President Wilson, horrified by Madero's murder, made removing Huerta from power his first order of business.

The United States supported several rebel groups that sprang up to challenge the Huerta government. Though the rebel bands of Pancho Villa and Emiliano Zapata became the best known, the most powerful and successful of the rebel commanders was Venustiano Carranza. After American forces seized the port of Vera Cruz, on the pretext that the Huerta government failed to apologize for the arrest of several American sailors, Carranza was best positioned to take advantage of the situation. Fatally weakened by the American occupation of Vera Cruz, Huerta fled the country and Carranza immediately moved his forces into Mexico City to seize power.

A short time later, the United States recognized the Carranza government. However, Carranza's former ally, Pancho Villa, was not happy with Carranza's rule. Villa immediately sent his men toward Mexico City to contest power. After losing several pitched battles against Carranza's forces, Villa retreated to the north, intent on prolonging the struggle. As a source of revenue and in retaliation for American support for Carranza, Villa began targeting American interests in northern Mexico. Though Villa committed a number of atrocities against Americans, including marching sixteen American miners off a train, stripping them naked, and then shooting them, it was the Columbus raid that finally forced Wilson's hand.

The president ordered Pershing to assemble all available troops in the area and pursue Villa into Mexico. It was a particularly sensitive mission, one for which Pershing was uniquely suited. As Washington saw the situation, action was required because the American people demanded it. However, policymakers also wanted to avoid war with Mexico all costs. It was impossible for the Wilson administration to remain idle after Villa's provocation without appearing impotent. However, more than Villa's capture or death, Wilson wanted border stability without having to fight a war. While many in Washington thought it would be a nice touch to actually capture or kill Villa, Pershing knew that this was only a secondary objective. His primary, more delicate, mission was to enter a friendly country with an invading army and to do so in such a way so as not to bring on a battle with the Mexican army, much less embroil the United States in a general war.

It was nearly an impossible mission. Pershing's force was going to be chasing an elusive enemy through some of the most hostile terrain on the planet, and could expect to be hated by virtually every person they encountered. Moreover, the Americans never knew when the Carranza government would order its army into the field to oppose them. The job at hand would require all of Pershing's tact, diplomacy, and soldierly abilities.

Within a week of the Columbus raid, Pershing crossed into Mexico and the pursuit was on. He brought with him a motley assortment of units and personnel. As his aide he had a new lieutenant, George S. Patton, who had literally camped outside Pershing's office. Every time Pershing walked by, Patton sprang to attention and begged to come along. After ignoring the eager lieutenant for two days, Pershing finally stopped to ask him why he should take him. Patton answered, "Because I want to go." Pershing coolly remarked that everyone wanted to go and dismissed Patton.

Flustered, Patton stammered: "But I want to go more than they do." Possibly remembering his own maneuvering to get into the Spanish-American War, Pershing relented and told Patton he could be his aide.

Patton soon joined Pershing's inner circle of confidants and, after the expedition was over, he introduced Pershing to his sister Nita. Although Nita was considerably younger than Pershing, they were soon romantically involved. Many, including Nita, thought that they would wed, and there are indications that Nita considered herself engaged to Pershing by the time he sailed for France to command the American Expeditionary Force in 1917. While Pershing was much taken with Nita, he was not prepared to embark on another great romance so soon after his wife's death. Under the demands of war and new romantic interests his ardor for Nita would rapidly cool.

Along with Patton, a number of other young officers were now learning their trade under Pershing, and many of them would have a major impact in future American wars. Among the future leaders were Courtney Hodges and William Simpson (both of whom would command field armies in World War II), Lesley McNair (commanding general of all army ground forces in World War II), and a young aviator, Carl Spaatz (the first chief of staff of the Air Force, after commanding the United States Army Air Force against Germany and then Japan).

Except for the addition of trucks to move supplies and a small air squadron, there was not much difference between the components of Pershing's expedition and the force General Miles led into Mexico in 1886. Once the aviators had wrecked the few obsolete planes assigned to the expedition, the differences were further lessened. Pershing even brought along an aged unit of Apache scouts, many of whom had helped Miles chase Geronimo through this same region. In a spectacular repetition of Miles' expedition, an American force once again entered Mexico guided by First Sergeant Chicken, on his seventh enlistment, and Hell Yet-Suey, chief of the

White Mountain Apache and notorious for disappearing when there was any work that needed to be done.[1]

For Pershing, the Mexican expedition involved deepening frustration. Hard-riding cavalry columns with equally hard-marching infantry regiments drove over 350 miles into Mexico, but continually just missed Villa. Although in one engagement Villa was wounded, he still managed to escape. Though Villa was never captured, Pershing did wreck Villa's military force. In a series of running battles, hundreds of Villa's soldiers were killed along with virtually all of his senior commanders.

As Pershing's expedition pushed deeper into Mexico, the hostility of the Mexican people and government grew. Inevitably, American troops got into tight situations with Carranza's National Army. When two of these meetings erupted into serious engagements with significant American casualties, it became apparent that the character of the operation was changing. Washington perceived what the Mexicans already believed. This was no longer an operation with limited aims. Pershing's expedition was rapidly turning into a full-scale invasion of a non-belligerent nation by the United States.

Even worse, it was beginning to resemble a struggle in which the United States might suffer serious embarrassments. Pershing's force was widely scattered and at the end of a very tenuous supply line. Moreover, as Pershing continued his search for Villa, large Mexican army forces began positioning themselves around the Americans, especially in the north, where they could strike across Pershing's line of communication. Even a cursory glance at an operations map revealed that the Mexican army was poised to sweep into Pershing's rear. After that it would only have been a matter of time until Pershing's force was routed or annihilated.

As they reviewed the situation, the War Department became convinced that the Carranza government had decided to try and humiliate the United States. To forestall this, Washington ordered five more regular regiments to the Mexican border and federalized the National Guard units of the border states. This concentration of close to 150,000 troops apparently convinced Carranza that a direct attack on Pershing's force was too risky, although he authorized small engagements and ambuscades. In the end, both governments understood exactly what had to happen. The United States had no alternative but to pull out. Yet, it had to save face in the process. In turn, Mexico realized it faced ruinous defeat if it tried to hasten that process unduly or forcibly. Turning to the time-tested methods of diplomacy, both countries appointed commissioners to decide how the United States would evacuate.[2]

While the commissioners debated, Pershing concentrated his forces at Colonia Dublan, not far from the border, in an area easy to supply. There he and his men settled down for six months, while the diplomats finished their discussions. During those six months, Wilson ordered the entire National Guard mobilized and sent to the border, to discourage any further insult to U.S. territory by Mexican raiders. All of these troops fell under Pershing, who was now commanding the largest army the United States had fielded since the Civil War.

The Mexican Expedition was not without benefits. First of all, it was an exacting field test for the entire regular army and the 150,000-man National Guard. For many of the officers this was the first time they had ever practiced the art of command in a real field environment. These now thoroughly trained regulars would provide the nucleus for the army the United States would field in World War I. It is doubtful that the first American units to see combat in France would have done as well as they did if the country had not had this pool of experienced veterans.

Moreover, operations in Mexico brought to light a number of serious deficiencies. Recruiting, for one, was far below what was projected and convinced many policymakers that, if America were to become involved in France, it would have to immediately institute a draft. It also became apparent that the Quartermaster Corps needed a thorough overhaul. If the quartermasters were straining every resource to deliver starvation-level rations to troops only a hundred miles from the U.S. border, how would they ever supply immense armies fighting thousands of miles from home? Finally, the army was forced to conduct operations without nearly enough of the implements of modern war: Trucks were in short supply and unreliable; the air squadron was so obsolete, it was out of the fight in less than a week; there were no modern machine guns and only a few inadequate radios. In summary, the Pershing expedition plainly demonstrated that the American army was not prepared to enter into a major global conflict, which, of course, is exactly what it did only a few months after Pershing marched his troops back over the border.

CHAPTER 7

Entry into World War I

IN 1916, WOODROW WILSON WAS ELECTED FOR HIS SECOND term on the slogan, "He kept us out of war," reflecting the public's desire to stay out of Europe's war. However, events were slowly converting public opinion. Though large segments of the U.S. population began favoring intervention, Wilson remained the most unwilling of warlords. By 1917 his repeated failures as a peacemaker convinced the president that, if America were to have a seat at future peace conference table, it would have to sacrifice on the battlefield. But Wilson was not one to get too far ahead of public opinion on such an issue. Since he was still vacillating, it would take something dramatic to force his hand toward war.

On January 22, 1917, Wilson made one more offer to act as a mediator of Europe's conflict, in his "Peace Without Victory" speech on the Senate floor. In response, Germany embarked on a number of measures, the strategic lunacy of which rivaled Hitler's decision to declare war on the United States while he was already bogged down before the gates of Moscow. First, at the end of January, Germany announced the resumption of unrestricted warfare and immediately began sinking U.S. flagged vessels. The United States promptly broke off formal relations with Germany and tensions rose to a boiling point. Seizing the moment, the British turned over to the Americans the famous Zimmerman Telegram from the German Foreign Minister to his ambassador in Mexico, which their famous "Room 40" code-breakers had intercepted. In it, the Germans suggested that Mexico join an alliance with Germany against the United States. If successful, the telegram stated, such an alliance would see Texas, New Mexico, and Arizona returned to Mexico. This supreme act of diplomatic incompetence aroused American popular anger against Germany to a fever pitch.

By the end of March, the country was ready for war and so was the president. On April 2, 1917, Wilson asked Congress to declare war and, by April 6, 1917, America was a belligerent in the "war to end all wars."

By the time America entered World War I, the killing had been going on for almost three years. From one end of Europe to the other, massive armies fought pitched battles on a previously unimaginable scale. The western front was a hellish tableau of struggling masses where gains were measured in yards and casualties were counted by the hundred thousand. Along 6,000 miles of trenches, millions of men eked out mole-like existences, battling not only the enemy, but also cat-sized rats, lice infestation, filth, and the constant fear they would be selected by fate to suffer a horrendous death.

By 1917, the blood of ten million men had already seeped into the ground, but the thirst for battle and slaughter among the Allied commanders remained unquenched. Just months before the United States entered the war, British Commander General Douglas Haig finally ordered a halt to his disastrous Somme offensive. In four months of fighting, Haig's men had advanced a mere two miles at a cost of almost 620,000 casualties, over 50,000 of them on the first day alone. Undeterred by the scale of the carnage, Haig immediately began planning new offensives at Ypres and Paschendale. Even if Haig was ready for a new round of bloodletting, the same was not true of Britain's political leadership. As he looked over the daily casualty reports, British Prime Minister David Lloyd George began to hold back new troop levies in Britain, rather than send them across the Channel to be fed into another of Haig's meat-grinder offensives.[1]

If Haig's ability to launch further offensives was temporarily stymied, French commanders were ready to pick up the slack. Despite having just survived a brutal battle of attrition at Verdun, the new French commander, General Robert Nivelle, declared the French army ready for renewed offensive action and launched his troops in a massive attack the same week that America declared war. A wiser man would have called off the assault almost immediately, as it was soon apparent that another disaster was unfolding. Unfortunately, Neville had bragged that he would tear through the German line in forty-eight hours and now he felt he had to produce. Instead of a rapid breakthrough on what he thought was a weak sector of the front, Neville found the Germans ready and waiting. Pushed forward with great élan, French troops ran into an unbroken defense boasting 100 heavy machine guns for every 1,000 meters of front. Under unrelenting fire, French battalions bogged down at their starting points. Only after losing 200,000 men did Neville admit defeat and call a halt.[2]

The French army, which was already teetering after Verdun, collapsed. While the first American troops prepared to sail to Europe, French soldiers mutinied. Before it was ended by the inspired leadership of General Philippe Petain, over sixty divisions had joined the mutiny and refused to conduct further offensives. In one famous incident, the French Second Division was ordered forward, only to arrive at the front drunk to a man and sans weapons.[3]

Such was the state of the Allied war effort on the eve of America's entry into the conflict. Unfortunately for the Allied cause, America was far from ready to undertake the course on which it had embarked, or to offer any prospect of immediate assistance. Even as Europe spent 1914 to 1917 in an apparent attempt to commit suicide, the United States, while welcoming Allied munitions' purchases (which by 1917 were running at an astronomical $250 million a month), had done little to prepare for its own possible entry into the war. In 1917 the entire American army was little more then a constabulary force of 127,588 men, with a further 80,446 in the National Guard.[4] For the past year most of this force had been patrolling the Mexican border with Pershing, unmindful that it would soon be involved in Europe's war. In light of the challenge ahead it was a puny force and Otto von Bismarck's comment about the British army could have been more appropriately directed at America. When asked what he would do if the British army landed on the Continent, Bismarck replied, "I shall send some Belgian police to arrest them."

When America entered the war, Pershing was still at Fort Sam Houston, Texas, far from the action in Washington. Determined not to be forgotten, Pershing set out to make his own destiny, as he had done upon America's declaration of war against Spain. On the day the United States declared war he dispatched two letters: one to Wilson and the second to Secretary of War Newton Baker. In the letter to Baker, Pershing wrote, "My life has been spent as a soldier, much of it on campaign, so that I am now fully prepared for the duties of this hour."[5] It was a not overly subtle way of telling the secretary that he was ready to serve and wanted to do so. At the time, Pershing was hopeful of commanding a division, and appears to have had no inclination or idea he was being considered for any higher position. What he was desperate to avoid was being stuck in a staff position in Washington, while others went off to war and glory.

Pershing's spirits were buoyed by a somewhat cryptic telegram from his father-in-law, Senator Warren, stating, "Wire me today whether and how much French you speak, read, and write." It was the first serious indication that Pershing was being considered for a command in France and, although he had always struggled with the French language, Pershing quickly responded that he was fluent. Soon after, further confirmation that he was being considered for a job in France came in a telegram from army chief of staff, General Hugh Scott, asking him to select four infantry regiments and an artillery regiment for service in Europe. The telegram also informed Pershing that if things worked out, he would receive command of the force.

On May 10, 1917, Pershing arrived in Washington and presented himself to Scott. Here he was formally told that he was to command the first division sent to France, but that no decision had been made on who would command the entire American Expeditionary Force (AEF). Pershing did not consider his chances of receiving overall command very high. He was a newly minted major general and there were several competent officers ahead of him in seniority: Leonard Wood, Franklin Bell, Thomas Barry, Hugh Scott, and Tasker Bliss.[6]

The decision as to who would command the entire AEF was in Secretary Baker's hands and it was one he earnestly wrestled with. He quickly eliminated for age and health reasons all but Wood and Pershing. Wood, however, presented a particular problem for Baker. He was the senior general in the army and had already been army chief of staff. He was also the best known and most admired man in the army, and his subordinates were fanatically loyal. Moreover, he was the darling of many politicians, a close friend of former President Teddy Roosevelt, an intimate of many congressmen, and a good friend to many of the East's financial elites. All of these people wanted Wood to command the AEF, and they fully expected his appointment.

But Wood also had major drawbacks. For one, though he expected total loyalty from his subordinates, he was never able to give it to those above him. Worse, he was incapable of keeping his mouth shut. Discretion just was not a concept that Wood was familiar with. Moreover, he had health problems relating to an accident when he was military governor of Cuba. Two operations had failed to alleviate his pain (a third one in 1927 killed him). Finally, while Wood had a vast range of military experience, he had never commanded a large force in the field. Of all the generals in the U.S. Army, only Pershing had ever commanded more then 10,000 men in active combat operations.

All of this weighed in Baker's decision, but in the end what finally counted Wood out was that he was known to have White House ambitions, and neither Baker nor the president thought they could count on his loyalty. Pershing might, and often did, disagree with his political masters, but in the final analysis he would follow orders and keep disagreements out of the newspapers. The lesson Pershing had absorbed before going off to fight in the Spanish-American War, when General Nelson Miles had been denied top command due to his political activities, was paying off.

Pershing's first meeting with the secretary of war went well and he left with a distinctly favorable impression of the secretary.[7] Newton Baker had himself been an unlikely choice for the position he occupied; he originally thought himself unsuited for the position. He had spent most of his life in municipal affairs, culminating as the mayor of Cleveland. His contact with Wilson had been mostly limited to having been a student of Wilson's when the future president taught at Johns Hopkins. So he was surprised when Wilson offered him the position. As he said at the time, "I never even played with tin soldiers." He came to Washington and explained to

Wilson that he knew nothing of military affairs, and because of his strong aversion to war, he was associated with several peace movements. Wilson heard him out and then asked if he was ready to be sworn in.[8]

It was an inspired choice, and Baker is rated among the finest secretaries of war in American history. He was well read and possessed of a methodical, quick-thinking mind. Although a small, timid-looking man, he was decisive in action, willing to take risks, and able to stand up to even the most severe pressure. He also had a philosophy of leadership that Pershing was to appreciate more and more. As Baker said after the war, "You select a commander in whom you have confidence; give him power and responsibility, and then work your head off to get him everything he needs and support him in every decision he makes."[9]

It was a code that Baker not only espoused, but lived by. During the war, a general Pershing had sent home approached Baker, wanting the secretary to ask Pershing why he had been removed. Baker refused, and told the general that Pershing must have absolute discretion in these matters, and that as secretary he would not interfere as long as Pershing delivered results. When the general insisted, Baker told him that by regulation he could demand a board of inquiry and that it would be scheduled for one month after the war ended. As General George Marshall later wrote to Pershing, "Though we have a hundred more wars, I do not think we will ever be so lucky in the choice of a Secretary."[10]

After weighing his selection, Baker called Pershing back for a second meeting to inform him that the president had decided that he would be commander-in-chief of the entire AEF. He should select an appropriate staff and leave for Europe as soon as possible.[11] Baker then told Pershing that that was the first of only two orders he would give him. The second would be "to come home."[12] In this subdued manner, Pershing was handed the most awesome responsibility the country had given a military commander since Grant took charge of all Union armies in 1864.

For the first time, Pershing had to face the reality that although America had drifted inexorably toward war for years, criminally little had been done to ready the nation. The National Defense Act, the "Plattsburg Movement," and past calls from President Roosevelt for mobilization had resulted in only a few extra militiamen. As for the army itself, it was in a pitiful condition, and completely unprepared for modern war. Except for the units on the Mexican border and a few scattered garrisons, the army existed only on paper, and even these paper legions looked woefully outdated. American ideas of war had far to go if the nation was to catch up with the scope and techniques of the slaughter in Europe.[13]

With little initial help, Pershing immediately undertook the creation of an American army. As a starting point, Pershing knew he would need a staff of superior talent to organize and manage the war. To get it, he insisted on being permitted to select the best men from throughout the army, as he considered most of the officers stationed in Washington inadequate. By contrast to what Pershing found in Washington, Germany went to war with a general staff of 650 of its best officers, specifically tasked to conduct all planning and coordinating necessary for a modern war. Even Britain, a relative newcomer to the idea of a general staff, started the war with 232 officers assigned to the task. The United States had a total of forty-one general staff officers, but by law no more than half of them were allowed in Washington, D.C. at any one time. Moreover, the quality of the men holding down staff jobs was far too low. As General George Marshall later said, "They were a collection of old officers who had ceased mental development years before . . . and were wholly unacquainted with the functions of a modern general staff."

This lack of an efficient staff helps explain how America found itself at war without any effective plan as to how to wage it. However, this was only part of the reason, as the president had ably abetted military incompetence. In 1916, President Wilson had summoned General Tasker Bliss to the Oval Office and coldly asked him if rumors he had heard that the army staff was preparing plans for a war with Germany were true. Bliss told him it was true and that the staff also prepared plans for wars with England, Japan, France, and Mexico as well. In a fury, Wilson demanded that such planning cease immediately and that every officer involved be transferred out of Washington. Although Wilson relented on the transfers, he effectively ensured that America went to war without any conception of how to mobilize, train, deploy, or fight its still nonexistent armies.[14]

The army Pershing assumed command of possessed none of the supplies or equipment necessary to fight a war. The United States could put only a handful of military planes in the air, and it boasted almost no aircraft factories. Although the massive artillery barrages on the western front were recounted daily in the news, virtually no preparations had been made to produce guns or shells on a large scale for an American army. And while British, French, and German armies relied on thousands of machine guns to cover their lines, American ordnance officers, in 1917, were still struggling to decide on which gun to adopt.[15]

The example of the air units will suffice to tell the story of the whole. A report from the War College had set an objective of 300 squadrons as the minimum necessary to support military operations. As for the Allies, they expected America to have 4,500 planes manned by 5,000 pilots in the field in 1918. Further, they fully expected the United States to produce over 30,000 aircraft a year for the Allied cause. Reality did not match such high hopes. In 1917, the army air service had all of sixty-five officers, only thirty-five of whom knew how to fly, and of these, only six were deemed physically capable of going to war. Furthermore, the army possessed a total of fifty-five planes, all used for training, of which fifty-one were obsolete and four archaic.

Pershing understood that the burden of building an American army fell squarely on his shoulders and that he could count on little initial help from the ossified, incompetent officers manning the woefully inefficient general staff. He also knew that he would have to train himself for the job and be prepared to alter his own attitudes and ideas to meet conditions he had never dreamed of encountering. His major task would be to become the army's organizer in chief. Like his hero, Grant, Pershing had to become an executive, a general presiding over a gigantic business enterprise. Divisions and corps were commanded, as they had always been, but armies were now managed. In this enlarged role Pershing's legal training and experience as governor of the Moro province would serve him well.[16]

Unable to rely on the existing general staff, Pershing immediately started selecting his own staff to accompany him to France. As a first step, he called in Major James Harbord and interviewed him to be his chief of staff. Harbord had worked his way up from the enlisted ranks with a combination of a quick, incisive mind and a capacity for hard work that only Pershing matched. During the short interview, Pershing asked Harbord if he spoke French. Told that he did not, Pershing said he needed a chief who spoke French and would take Harbord in another capacity. Later, Pershing handed Harbord a list with two other names he was considering for the position and asked him who would be best for the job. Harbord glanced at the names and then informed Pershing that he thought himself better qualified than the other two men. Pershing had his chief.[17]

Together, Pershing and Harbord selected thirty other officers who would accompany them to France. During their search, Pershing was deluged with requests to accompany him from friends, acquaintances, and even strangers. Most he pushed off with a compliment, a smile, and a handshake, but one was particularly vexing—former President Theodore Roosevelt. The old Rough Rider had thrilled the nation with his offer to raise a volunteer division and lead it to France. However, Pershing and Baker were solidly against the formation of volunteer units, which had proven time and again to be administrative nightmares, and the offer was politely refused. But Pershing both liked and respected Roosevelt. He also considered himself in Roosevelt's debt for his promotion to general and was greatly troubled to have to refuse Roosevelt's offer and quash his hopes for a combat command. Pershing was therefore elated when Roosevelt abandoned his plans for a major combat command, opting instead to congratulate Pershing on his selection to command the AEF and asking if he could find positions for his two sons, a major and captain in the Officers' Reserve Corps.[18] This was something Pershing was only too happy to do for his old friend.

Even after selecting his staff, there were a number of administrative issues that he had to handle before he could depart for Europe. His most pressing concern was quashing the idea that the United States should not waste time creating an army. Rather, many believed the nation should just send raw recruits to Europe for use as replacements in shot-up British and French units. At the time the word used for this policy was "amalgamation," and it was to haunt Pershing throughout the war. Within days of the United States declaring war, senior French and British officials visited with the president and the secretary of war and pushed the amalgamation issue hard. The British wanted 500,000 draftees immediately sent to their depots for training and then used as replacements for their depleted units. It was a bold demand given that the British government was already deliberately starting to hold new recruits in Britain rather than see them massacred in further useless offensives. The French, on the other hand, did not specify an exact number of recruits they wanted for their divisions, but only asked for all that could be sent.[19]

For Pershing, the idea of amalgamation was anathema. If American soldiers were going to bleed and die in defense of another nation they were going to do so under American commanders and their own flag; national honor demanded nothing less. He was gratified to discover the president was of a like mind. After watching the terrible bloodletting in Europe, Wilson entered the war convinced that the "old order" was corrupt and that it was up to America to establish a new, and more just international system. Wilson and Baker quickly perceived that the French and British were hoping to win the war with American blood, but without independent American combat forces so that when peace talks began they would be free to ignore Wilson's views. The president fully understood that his status in any future peace talks would grow or diminish in direct relation to Allied perceptions of the efforts and successes of an independent American army. He therefore informed the Allies that American troops would fight only as an independent army, reminding them that when Louis XVI sent a French army to fight with Washington, he ordered General Rochambeau to insure that French soldiers fought as an independent force.[20]

However, this was far from the end of the amalgamation issue, and Pershing was glad he left for France carrying an order approved by the president and signed by Baker that made it possible for him to resist continuous pressure on the issue. This pressure would become almost overwhelming as the Allies came close to losing the war in 1918, but Pershing, always referring to his written instructions, remained steadfast. The critical paragraph five of Wilson's instructions read:

> In military operations against the Imperial German Government you are directed to cooperate with the forces of other countries employed against the enemy; but in doing so the underlying idea must be kept in view that the forces of the United States are a separate and distinct component of the combined forces, the identity of which must be preserved. This fundamental rule is subject to such minor exceptions in particular circumstances as your

judgment may approve. The decision as to when your command, or any of its parts, is ready for action is confided to you, and you will exercise full discretion in determining the manner of cooperation.[21]

It was the kind of order that Pershing might have written himself, and there is widespread suspicion he was the actual author.

As May drew to a close, Pershing sailed for France on the S.S. *Baltic*. With him was his new staff and enlisted support persons—192 in all. Many of these staff officers would become division and corps commanders later in the war and some would have spectacular careers in the next war, including Captain George S. Patton, who continued as Pershing's aide. Among the well-wishers at the pier was Patton's sister Nita. She was fussing over Pershing, and their relationship had blossomed to the point that rumors floated freely about an "after the war" marriage.

The crossing was uneventful, though many lost sleep as the ship began a regular zigzag pattern, alerting its passengers that they had entered the U-boat killing grounds. Pershing used the time to start planning the creation of an American army and with Harbord began considering serious questions about staff organization, port and rail capacity, the speed with which troops could be shipped from the United States, and the hundreds of other details that could mean the difference between success and failure in battle. It was during these discussions that Pershing decided that effective operations required at least a million men, which was double what Washington was planning. Even this figure was only half of what was eventually required for victory. Harbord later said of the experience, "Our war ideas were expanding as we neared the theater. Officers whose lives have been spent trying to avoid spending fifteen cents of Government money now confronted the necessity of expending fifteen billions of dollars—and on their intellectual and professional expansion depended their avoidance of the scrap heap."[22]

Pershing, for his part, never hesitated to consign officers who did not measure up with his standards to professional oblivion. General Robert Bullard, who once considered Pershing weak, a pacifist in uniform, told an assembled group of officers, "Pershing intends to build an army and he wants only results. He will crush anyone who gets in his way and ruin anyone who disappoints him." It was not a gentle approach to war management, but it did produce what Pershing demanded—results.

*Pershing, Capt John J.
15th Cavalry--Moro
Conqueror in
Mindanao—circa
1901*

General Sumner and Pershing meeting with Moro Sultans—circa 1902

Mrs. Pershing—circa 1905

MRS. J.J. PERSHING

Pershing and family in the Philippines—circa 1912

Pershing and his son Warren—circa 1914

Pershing at his Casa Grandes Base in Mexico—circa 1916

Pershing pays his respects at Lafayette's Tomb—circa 1917

*General Pershing arrives in
France—circa 1917*

Savior of the French Army, General Petain meets with Pershing in 1917

left   British Expeditionary Force Commander - General Haig meets with Pershing in 1917

below   Pershing talking to 4th Divsion just before it shipped back to the United States in March 1919

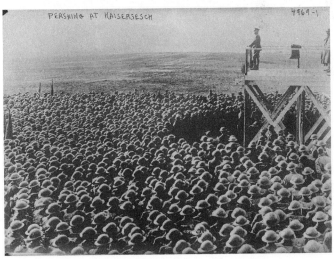

Pershing visits Arlington Cemetary circa 1921

CHAPTER 8

The Americans Arrive

ON JUNE 9, 1917, THE MORNING AFTER PERSHING ARRIVED in London, he and his key staff were ushered into the presence of King George V, whom Pershing found entertaining and well informed. At one point, the king pulled him aside to show how he had converted Buckingham Palace's gardens into a potato farm. Here, the king complained about the German terror bombing of London and, pointing at a statue of Queen Victoria, exclaimed, "The god-damned Kaiser even tried to blow up his own Grandmother."

Amid a whirlwind of social events that Pershing greatly resented, but found impossible to avoid, he found time to meet with and be briefed on every facet of the war by the British Imperial Staff. Everyone was anxious to get American soldiers into the war and more than once Pershing had to sidestep the amalgamation issue. Meeting with the chief of the Imperial General Staff, General William Robertson, Pershing asked about the possibility of getting some British ships to help move American troops to France. Pershing was soon to discover that except for the fights over amalgamation, no other issue would bring the Allied cause closer to rupture than shipping. Pershing was taken aback when Robertson categorically refused to allocate British shipping to the United States, stating that Britain was having problems finding sufficient shipping to meet its own needs.

The next day, Pershing met with Prime Minister Lloyd George, and again he brought up the question of using British tonnage to ship American troops. When Lloyd George told him the extent of British losses to U-boats, Pershing was shocked. Over 1.5 million tons of shipping had been lost in the month of April alone, and new production had replaced only a small fraction of that total. Pershing realized that the success of the war would rest on shipping, and at the moment matters were looking bleak. He also knew that if America had to rely solely on its own shipping resources, it would take three years to move a million men to France. Sobered, Pershing took leave of his London hosts and left for France without resolving critical cross-Atlantic transport issues.[1]

+⇥═⇤+

Pershing's arrival in Paris was tumultuous, as the French, in desperate need of America's help, gave full vent to their emotions. Tens of thousands of the war-weary packed every space along the wide boulevards and squares and slowed his convoy's progress to a crawl. Pershing called it the most touching and, in a sense, the most pathetic demonstration he had ever witnessed. It brought home to him, as nothing else could, just how desperate the French were to be rescued by the American armies.[2]

French morale was at a low point. The disastrous offensives of General Nivelle had ended in another shattering French battlefield defeat. The arrogant Nivelle, who boasted he could break the German line at will and do it within forty-eight hours, had instead broken the will of the French army and sacrificed another 200,000 men for no gain.[3]

As soon as possible, Pershing went to visit General Philippe Petain and learned the true extent of the French crisis. Petain had replaced Nivelle when mutinies broke out, and through a combination of compassion, toughness, and wise concessions, he saved France. When Pershing sat down with him, he learned that sixteen full corps had laid down their arms and refused to go forward, as if issued a simultaneous order to do so. Petain also informed him that there had been very little bloodshed during these mutinies, and only rare instances of men abusing their officers. Rather, said Petain, there was just a unanimous outcry of: "We have had enough! Down with the war! We will not go into the line!" As Pershing and Petain met, the mutinies were still in progress, but waning. Throughout this first meeting, Petain was somber, but forthcoming in a way that deeply impressed Pershing.[4] It was the beginning of a life-long friendship.

As Pershing lunched with Petain's staff on June 16, Petain announced that the French army could no longer conduct anything but the most limited offensives and admitted, "We must wait for the Americans." Soon after this announcement, the conversation turned to other topics, but Petain remained silent, apparently lost in thought. After some time had passed in relaxed conversation Petain suddenly interjected, "I hope it is not too late." Pershing stared at his host and for the first time understood just how close the war was to being lost.[5]

Pershing returned to Paris, where he resided and worked in a mansion that a rich American, Ogden Mills, had placed at his disposal for the war's duration. There was much to be done, and Pershing plunged ahead, often taking an inordinate interest in even the minutest items. When Harbord told him he should save his energies for the important things, Pershing informed him that he wanted everyone on the staff to understand how his mind worked. He was fully aware that whatever he did now would set the pattern for the AEF for the rest of the war.[6]

Harbord has left us a contemporary portrait of his boss at work:

> He thinks very clearly and directly; goes to his conclusions directly upon matter needing a decision. He can talk straighter to people when calling them down than anyone I have ever seen. He has a naturally good disposition and a keen sense of humor. He loses his temper occasionally, and stupidity and vagueness irritate him more than anything else. He can stand plain talk, but the staff officer who goes in with only vagueness where he ought to have certainty, who does not know what he wants, and fumbles about, has lost time and generally gained some straight talk. He develops a great fondness for people he likes and is indulgent toward their faults, but at the same time is relentless when convinced of inefficiency. Personal loyalty to friends is strong with him, but does not blind him to the truth.

Pershing had a couple of big questions to answer. At what ports would the American troops arrive, and which would they then use for logistical support? Where would he build the great depots his planned million-man army would require? Where would the American army fight? The British wanted the Americans to come through the Channel ports and establish themselves behind their own lines. However, Pershing's staff had surveyed these ports and found that they were working at full capacity to support the British and that the rail net in the area was already strained to the point of collapse. Just as important to his decision not to use the Channel ports was Pershing's awareness of British sensitivity over their forces being the ones guarding the Channel ports, in the event they had to make a hasty exit from the Continent. The British would not let the American army have its own sector on this critical part of the front, and Pershing recognized the British offer of training support and bases behind their lines for what it was—a back door to amalgamation at a later date.

Immediately to the south of the British, the French armies guarded the doorway to Paris. This was a sacred duty to the French and only their army would be allowed to cover this sector. So, with few other choices available, Pershing selected Lorraine as the American army sector and the St. Mihiel salient as his army's first objective. The Lorraine sector had several important advantages. First, it provided the Americans with use of three deep-draft Atlantic ports not already overtaxed by the war: St. Nazaire, La Pallice, and Bassens. Second, the rail nets from these ports to the front, while not ideal, were in better shape than those in any other area of France. Furthermore, the Lorraine sector had been relatively quiet for most of the war and therefore the local supplies, on which the American army would rely to complement those shipped from America, were not yet exhausted. Finally, from Pershing's viewpoint, the Lorraine sector presented one priceless advantage; an advance of only forty miles would cut the main German supply line at Thionville and could dislocate the entire German position and precipitate a general withdrawal. Such an advance would place the American army squarely on German soil and on top of the critical Saar coal fields and the iron mines of Longwy-Briey.[7]

Pershing went to see Petain, and in a few hours they had hammered out an arrangement. The American army would have the Lorraine sector, as soon as there was an American army.

On June 26, 1917, fourteen thousand men of the First Division arrived at St. Nazaire. Their arrival left Pershing singularly unimpressed. To his expert eye the soldiers were undisciplined and poorly trained. Many of their uniforms did not fit and most were fresh from recruiting stations, with little training other than basic drill. Most of their company commanders and other junior officers had been in the army for less than six months, while the army had siphoned off most of the long-serving regular officers and sergeants just before deployment, to form cadres for the new divisions.

Pershing was also far from impressed by the First Division's commander, Major General William L. Sibert. Sibert was an engineer, promoted largely for his outstanding work helping to build the Panama Canal. He had never commanded combat troops, was not a driver of men, and to Pershing's eye he did not look like a soldier. Sibert failed Pershing's first-impression test, which was almost universally fatal to any senior AEF officer's career. Unless he found a way to impress the boss, Sibert was destined for elimination. For the moment, however, Pershing had other worries. Sibert had strong political support in Washington, which Pershing, new to supreme power, was not yet prepared to test.

Fortunately, there were some officers in the First Division whom Pershing knew and held in high esteem. He did not hesitate to move them into positions of authority. Hanson Ely rose to command the Fifth Division; George Duncan, the Eighty-Second; and Frank Parker, the First. Harold Fiske later took charge of all AEF training and Arthur L. Conger was to become one of the AEF's foremost intelligence officers. There were two other officers in the First Division worthy of note. One was barely known to Pershing before the war but eventually became the operations officer for the American First Army and proved himself a planning and organizational genius—George C. Marshall. Despite a rather rough introduction to each other, Pershing was later to say that Marshall was the finest officer in the AEF. In turn, Marshall considered Pershing a true friend and the epitome of what a soldier should be. The other officer, Peyton March, was the commander of the First Division's artillery. Pershing soon put him in charge of all AEF artillery, and although March grated many staff officers, Pershing thought highly of him and often called him to his headquarters for lengthy private conferences on the general state of AEF affairs. The two men had a strong professional relationship, but not a personal one.

It soon broke down and became stormy when in March 1918, Baker recalled March to become army chief of staff.

March, unlike his predecessors, was a strong chief of staff who had zero interest in soothing feelings or gathering a consensus on important decisions. As one staff officer said, "He took hold of the Army staff as a dog does to a cat and shook it." Another officer explained March's methods of leadership: "He did not work out problems with people—he ordered. He was the War Department."[8]

When March arrived at the War Department the backlog of troops awaiting training and shipment to France had reached scandalous proportions. To fix it, March had to do two things: snap the War Department out of its lethargy and break the power of the bureau chiefs. Despite the creation of the chief of staff position, these chiefs still reigned supreme over private fiefdoms, such as the Ordnance and Quartermaster Departments, where they would brook no interference. March attacked both problems with relentless zeal and callous personal brutality. All who opposed him were crushed. Bureau chiefs were relieved, other senior bureau personnel had their powers constrained, while officers hand-selected by March flooded into reorganized staff sections.

Dissatisfied with the Quartermaster Department, March decided to reorganize logistics and put the builder of the Panama Canal, General George Goethals, in charge. March then called in the former chief of the Quartermaster Department and curtly told him, "I have cut off your head and order you out of the War Department."[9]

For March, winning the war consisted of one main thing. Pershing needed troops and materiel for the great offensives that were then just beginning, and March was determined to provide them. During the eight months of the war that March was in charge of the War Department, the army doubled in size to 3.7 million men, and more than 1.8 million men went to France. When Bernard Baruch, whom President Wilson had placed in charge of coordinating American industry during the war, questioned March about the capacity of the ship transports and the French railroads' ability to carry the numbers of men March was pushing to the embarkation points, March bluntly responded, "We'll pack them in like sardines," and "What did God give them feet for?"

Pershing could see the results of what March was accomplishing, but this failed to prevent a falling out. Conflict was perhaps inevitable between two competent, strong-minded men, each with different convictions of the other's role. Pershing saw his position as akin to General Ulysses S. Grant, who commanded all Union Armies in the field and used the chief of staff, General Henry Halleck, as a subordinate who stayed in Washington to coordinate and support Grant's decisions. Pershing was reinforced in this perception by prior chiefs of staff, who fell easily into a subordinate role. March, however, saw the War Department as the head of a national effort, of which Pershing's AEF was only a part.

Pershing also became convinced that March was angling to replace him, an idea that Harbord (no fan of March's) constantly fed. Soon March and Pershing were violently arguing over promotions and Pershing began seeing something sinister behind the inevitable mistakes and delays involved with moving millions of men and millions of tons of equipment across the Atlantic. Though March was subjected to unstinting criticism from Pershing and gave as good as he got, a more balanced opinion would be that both men were in the right place at the right time and that the war would probably have lasted at least another year if either had been absent.

In the meantime, the First Division had arrived in France, and the French people needed to see American troops. Accordingly, the Sixteenth Regiment was selected to march through the streets of Paris in a Fourth of July celebration. Pershing, who was not impressed with the unit's soldierly qualities, was reluctant to approve the march, but was prevailed on to recognize its necessity. As the U.S. soldiers marched, Pershing cringed at the thought of the discerning eyes of Allied officers unfavorably judging his men. He should not have worried. All the French saw that day were incredibly large men brimming with confidence and anxious to get into the fight, so unlike the dispirited, weakened, and often cringing French soldiers of 1917. Here was an army that had never tasted defeat.

When the parade ended at Picpus Cemetery, the burial site of the Marquis de Lafayette, huge throngs gathered to hear the oratory. One after another, French speakers heaped praise on the Americans. Even Pershing, never at ease as a public speaker, said a few words, but soon ceded the duty to a staff officer and accomplished speaker, Colonel C. E. Stanton. Stanton rose to give America's formal comment to the French people:

> What we have in blood and treasure are yours. In the presence of your illustrious dead we pledge our hearts and our honor in carrying this war to a successful conclusion.
> Lafayette we are here!

CHAPTER 9

Building an Army

APPRECIATION FOR THE AMERICAN EXPERIENCE IN WORLD
War I requires an understanding of two basic concepts. First, that
this was a war radically different then anything that had come before it; second, that Pershing had a different approach to fighting it
than did his Franco-British Allies.

World War I was truly the first war of the masses, who were
armed to the teeth by the governments of highly industrialized
countries. It is difficult to underestimate the effects that rapid industrialization had on the conduct of warfare. For instance, France
was able to mobilize over 20 percent of its total population for
war—several times the percentage Napoleon's levee-en-masse had
gathered to his banners. Moreover, industrialization, widening and
increasing the scale of militaries, had eliminated the possibility of
victory in one great decisive battle. Within living memory, the

Prussians had been able to crush Austrian military power at Sadowa (also called the Battle of Königgrätz) in 1866, and humiliate France's Napoleon III at the Battle of Sedan in 1870. Now, generals could only dream of striking that one crushing blow that would bring glory and victory in one fell swoop.

The new reality of war was bleak. Industrial armies were so large that they could absorb massive bloodletting and still remain viable. Efficient mass mobilizations provided armies with the ability to absorb losses in the hundreds of thousands, and later in the millions, and still maintain themselves as efficient fighting forces. Additionally, modern armies possessed remarkable regenerative capacity, as industrial economies were quick to replace materiel losses as well.

Until 1918, opposing armies had only one method to defeat an enemy able to absorb large numbers of casualties and still bring additional reserves forward to counterattack: attrition. When America entered the war, the deadly calculus of attrition-based warfare was turning decidedly against the Allies. Russia had collapsed into anarchy and numerous German divisions were ready to redeploy from the Eastern to the Western Front. It was anyone's guess whether America could get enough men and equipment to Europe in time to reverse the situation.

Rapid industrialization not only allowed for the support of massive armies, it also introduced advanced technologies and weapons systems to the battlefield in numbers that would have been unfathomable to commanders in any previous war. Prior to Pickett's Charge, at the Battle of Gettysburg, Lee tried to break the Union line with a mere 170 guns. In contrast, during World War I, it was not uncommon for attacks to be supported by 5,000 artillery pieces. At Waterloo, Wellington had fired less then 10,000 rounds of artillery ammunition. At the Somme, Haig fired almost two million shells in preparatory fires alone. When the war began, Allied councils feared they could never match the $70 million in gold reserves Germany had set aside and kept in Spandau Castle specifically to finance any future war. By 1915, the Allies were spending that amount every twelve hours during a big push, and every two days when the front was quiet.

Artillery, which could now be fired with great accuracy from tens of miles away, dominated the World War I battlefield. But from the trench line to about 2,000 meters out the machine gun reigned supreme. At many parts of the front, armies had over one hundred machine guns per thousand yards of front. With cyclic rates of fire of over 500 rounds per minute, nothing could survive for long within the beaten zone of interlocked machine guns. Together, rapid-fire artillery and machine guns brought the lethality of modern war to unimagined levels. To escape this lethal combination, soldiers from Switzerland to the English Channel burrowed deep into the ground, as after 1914 the war stalemated into a series of bloody battles of attrition.

Generals raised in the Napoleonic tradition had no answer to this new form of warfare except to keep battering their opponents and hope the other side would quit first. After the war J. F. C. Fuller lambasted this lack of intellectual innovation in his widely distributed pamphlet, *Generalship, Its Diseases and Cures.* Fuller popularized the idea of "Château Generals" who never left luxurious manor homes as they ordered men to their deaths by the thousands. What Fuller failed to mention is that France and England each suffered over seventy generals killed in action and many more wounded. This is not the record of men who did not care about how their soldiers' lives were expended. Rather, it demonstrates that many were professionals who were often running risks at least as great as any private, as they fruitlessly sought answers that would relieve the never-ending carnage.

Unable to find tactical solutions, the generals turned to industry and technology for answers. First, the Germans introduced poison gas to the battlefield. But while gas added a horrendous new nightmare to the life of the frontline soldier, it failed to break the stalemate. Next came the tank, which was impervious to machine guns and could roll over barbed wire. It was truly a weapon of promise, which in the next war would return mobility to the battlefield. However, in World War I, despite promising early successes, the tank proved too slow and cumbersome to make a decisive difference.

Although generals understood that recent inventions were changing war, they had no reference points to guide them over unfamiliar terrain. Generals who came of age when muscle power (both human and animal) dictated the extent and pace of military operations could not fathom the requirements of operations in a world of internal combustion engines, wireless radios, aircraft, and new weapons like poison gas. Figuring out the answers would have to wait until a new set of interwar military thinkers such as Heinz Guderian, J. F. C. Fuller, and Basil Liddell Hart created the innovative doctrinal systems popularly known as Blitzkrieg warfare.

Pershing, firmly entrenched in the traditions of American warfare, had his own ideas as to what was required. His first instinct was to assume that U.S. forces would bring an innate moral and physical superiority to the battlefield, which would transcend the need to master the "irrelevant" arts of trench warfare. He believed that superior individual marksmanship would counter the machine gun and that the path to victory was through getting out of the trench systems and returning to "open warfare." Pershing remained convinced that once American forces were employed in mass they would rapidly crack the German trench line and force the enemy into a war of movement.

A war of ideas soon raged within the AEF between those who adhered to the traditional, human-centered ideas of the prewar army and those who increasingly appreciated the modern, industrial ideas more prevalent in the European armies. The former set of ideas—based on infantry manpower, the rifle and bayonet, simple attack plans, the maximization of maneuver, and the hope of decisive operational and even strategic results—was summed up in the phrase "open warfare." The latter set of ideas—based on the integration of the latest weaponry, the use of meticulously prepared attack plans, the maximization of firepower, and methodical attacks aimed at specific enemy units to achieve more modest operational results—was often called "trench warfare." With a few notable exceptions, American officers in 1917 were committed to the ideal of open warfare, but interaction with veteran Allied officers and their own experiences on the front lines in 1918 gave rise to a new appreciation of the ideas and methods associated with the competing doctrine of trench warfare.[1]

It is not easy to reconcile Pershing's conceptions of how to fight the war with the reality of the battlefield in 1917. In truth, no one seemed to understand what Pershing really meant by open warfare and in April 1918 Major General Hunter Liggett wrote to general headquarters to inform them that he could find nothing in the mass of literature his corps had been issued explaining how his commanders were to prepare units for open warfare. Even when bitter experience should have altered battlefield perceptions, Pershing persisted in demanding that units continue to train for open warfare.

For instance, in six weeks of fighting at Belleau Wood, the Second Division, whose starting strength had been 28,000 men, suffered 13,719 losses. Only when the unit gave up its reliance on the rifle as the supreme weapon on the battlefield and adopted attritional rolling artillery barrages was it able to gain ground and reduce its loss rate. Nevertheless, the AEF staff study of that battle baselessly concluded: "the rifle again proved to be the chief weapon of the infantry and the regulation methods of handling artillery in open warfare were found to be sound and capable of execution."[2]

Of course, the British and French trainers who staffed the AEF training camps had another conception of how war should be fought. They eschewed practice with rifles in favor of grenades, trench mortars, and the other, more relevant, instruments required to kill and survive in the trenches. Pershing continually railed against this kind of instruction, which he was convinced was sapping the offensive spirit and morale of American soldiers. Since the 1960s a number of revisionist historians have severely criticized Pershing on this score. They claim that the AEF was often inadequately trained, poorly supplied, and inconsistently led.

The truth is that in the few detailed analyses actually done of AEF combat effectiveness, American units come off rather well. A detailed look at the 165th Infantry Regiment's tactical performance in over 180 days in the trenches demonstrates the rapid absorption and modification of French doctrine; coordinated combined arms operations on defense and offense; and attacks across no man's land that used fire and movement to overwhelm German defenses. A veteran described one of the regiment's late summer attacks as a case study in decentralized infantry tactics:

> The battalion breaks up into companies as it gets nearer the front; and the companies, when they reach the point where they are likely to be under shell-fire, separate into platoons with considerable distance between them. In action, men advance with generous intervals between. When they get close to the enemy the advance is made by frequent rushes, about a fourth of the men in a platoon running forward, while their comrades keep the enemy's heads down by their fire, until all of them can get close. In its last stages the warfare of these small groups is more like Indian fighting. . . . To take machine gun nests—I am not speaking of regularly wired and entrenched positions, which is the business of artillery to reduce before the infantry essays them—it is often a matter of individual courage and strategy. . . . Often the resistance is overcome by some daring fellow who works his way across hollows which are barely deep enough to protect him from fire, or up a gully or watercourse, until he is near enough to throw hand grenades. Then it is all over.[3]

This is hardly a description of soldiers or commanders who were not prepared for war on the western front. What it does describe is something unique to the American character and the American army—a strong sense of pragmatism. At all levels of command, officers and soldiers digested what Franco-British trainers were saying, along with what AEF headquarters was propounding. When units entered battle, commanders picked what worked best from both sources, adjusted their methods accordingly, and performed spectacularly. It is unfortunate for the reputation of the AEF that too many historians have accepted the judgments of European writers and soldiers about the effectiveness of the American army without doing detailed studies of their own or questioning what interest Europeans had in minimizing the contribution of the AEF.

In truth, Pershing just did not have much time to get involved in the training of divisions and regiments. He had to entrust that duty to the men who commanded them and to let them get on with it. On the other hand, Pershing had an eagle-eye for units that were not measuring up to his high standards and felt no compunction about letting commanders know of his displeasure, with usually terminal consequences to that subordinate's future command prospects. At one point, Pershing's penchant toward on-the-spot corrections led to a famous incident between Pershing and Captain George Marshall.

In early October 1917, Pershing went to watch Major Theodore Roosevelt Jr., the former president's son, demonstrate a new method for attacking a fortified position. Afterward, Pershing asked Sibert, the division commander, to present a critique. Sibert stumbled and appeared unsure of himself, causing Pershing to explode and begin dressing down Sibert in front of his subordinates. The division chief of staff tried to intercede, but he in turn also gave ill-informed or evasive answers and was likewise forced to endure Pershing's withering scorn.

As Pershing finished, Captain Marshall, who was loyal to Sibert, stepped up to explain, but Pershing was not willing to listen and turned away. Marshall reached out and put a hand on his arm. "General Pershing, there's something to be said here and I think I should say it. . . ." Marshall then angrily went on about the difficulties the division was encountering daily and what they were doing to overcome them. Horrified observers stood mute, convinced that Marshall was in the process of destroying what, until that moment, had been a promising military career. When he was done, Pershing silently appraised Marshall and replied, "You must appreciate the troubles we have." Still upset, Marshall replied, "Yes General, but we have them every day and they have to be solved before night."

Friends fully expected Marshall to be fired. But Pershing was not the kind of man to take honest, forthright criticism personally. On subsequent visits to the First Division, Pershing would purposely seek Marshall out and pull him aside to ask how things were going. Marshall later commented, "You could talk to him as if you were discussing somebody in the next country. He never held it against you for an instant. I never saw another commander like that. It was one of his great strengths that he could listen to things."[4] When it came time to establish the First Army, Pershing remembered the competent captain and promoted him to be the First Army's operations officer.[5] Sibert, on the other hand, was relieved soon afterward. Pershing was not going to let a man who could not critique a battalion training exercise command a division in combat.

During these early months, Pershing was monumentally overworked. He was trying to form an army, and lengthy visits to Haig's and Petain's headquarters made him fully aware of the truly massive scope of the undertaking. In his first visits both commanders greeted him warmly, Haig particularly so, as he was ecstatic that the British cabinet had approved his plans for a great new offensive at Passchendaele, a name that was soon to become synonymous with mud and slaughter.

Following the lead of the Allies, Pershing expanded his staff and reorganized it into the G–1 (Personnel), G–2 (Intelligence), G–3 (Operations), and G–4 (Logistics) structure recognizable to today's officers. He also recognized that he had to get himself and his staff out of the trap of Paris. While they were in the capital, it was almost impossible to avoid social engagements with important dignitaries, and it was much too easy for visitors to drop in. All of which cost Pershing the one thing that was in shortest supply—time. His aide recorded at the time, "The general is raving mad and swears he will get out of Paris as soon as possible."

On September 6, Pershing moved his headquarters 150 miles outside of Paris, to the town of Chaumont. It was near the likely American sector and had ample office space and billeting for his enlarged staff. When Pershing first looked the site over, every local person he met told him that he could not make a better choice. Only the local French military commander made a strong case for Pershing to look elsewhere, and it took a few moments for Pershing to appreciate that the French officer was afraid he would lose his comfortable accommodations if the Americans moved into town. He was right.

Militarily, Pershing's most pressing, and seemingly insurmountable, problems revolved around logistics. Small issues, such as U.S.-based quartermasters wasting tonnage by sending over lawnmowers and other useless items, were an annoyance. But what was really slowing the American war effort to a crawl was the lack of a well-organized rear zone for logistics or an efficient purchasing program to obtain as much materiel as possible within Europe, thereby freeing up trans-Atlantic shipping capacity.

The AEF would, by the end of 1918, consist of nearly two million men consuming 45,000 tons of supplies a day. To organize this effort, Pershing created a scheme for the "lines of communications," which was divided into Base, Intermediate, and Advanced sections. He insisted that the Base (of which there would eventually be eight locations) hold forty-five days' worth of supplies, the Intermediate thirty days, and the Advanced fifteen days.[6] This meant that dozens of large depots needed to be built; railroads across central France required reconditioning, and in many cases they needed to be built from scratch; and wharves, along with thousands of warehouses, needed to be constructed. Additionally, thousands of trucks and tens of thousands of beasts of burden would have to be found to move everything from the railheads to the troops.

It was a monumental task, which Pershing, given all of his other duties, could not handle on his own. He looked long and hard for a man tough enough for the job and who could bear up to responsibilities almost as great as Pershing's own. He finally settled on Brigadier General Richard Blatchford, an old friend who had performed well for Pershing in Mexico. Pershing gave Blatchford the authority to do whatever he thought necessary. Unfortunately, in a short time Blatchford proved unfit for the job, and Pershing replaced him with Major General Francis Kernan. Hoping to ease an old friend's feelings, Pershing told Blatchford he was not being removed for incompetence, but only because he was needed back in the United States to help train a combat unit and then redeploy it back to France. After the war, Blatchford considered his removal a blemish on his reputation and pushed the matter up to the secretary of war. Pershing, who was then army chief of staff, wrote him:

> I have refrained from going into this because of our lifelong friendship for you and my reluctance to say anything that might be disagreeable. The truth is, however, that in the position in which you were assigned your services were not satisfactory and did not warrant your retention on the very important duty involved. . . . It might have been better to have advised you at the time.[7]

Before long, Kernan too proved a disappointment and by July 1918, when Pershing issued orders to form the First American Army, logistics were in a sorry state. Things were so bad that reports about massive bottlenecks at the ports and inefficient logistical administration were reaching Washington. Many in the capital were convinced that Pershing took on too much work himself and was becoming overextended. Colonel Edward House, an intimate and chief advisor to President Wilson, and the army chief of staff, General March, both approached Secretary Baker to suggest that a new man be sent over to take care of all rear areas so Pershing could focus on training and fighting.

Baker agreed with this assessment and sent a letter to Pershing saying that he was going to send General George Goethals to France to take over logistics in a coordinate, rather than subordinate, position.[8] At this time, Goethals was the number two man at the War Department and proving to be a brilliant logistician, with a particular talent for packing more materiel on a cargo ship than anyone thought possible. Pershing, however, did not take Baker's note well and wrote back that this new command scheme violated the fundamental principle of unity of command. He insisted that only one person must be responsible for the entire war effort or risk confusion, chaos, and ultimate failure. He did not protest Goethals' arrival by name, but insisted that whoever controlled logistics be subordinate to him. Fortunately, Baker, who was always deferential to his field commander, agreed to take no action until he and Pershing were in full accord.

Pershing already knew that his logistical arrangements were in chaos, and even though he had not protested the choice of Goethals, he abhorred the idea that Washington would select a person for so critical a role in his theater. He needed a man who could get the job done, but who was also Pershing's man. Twice he had put men in charge and given them extraordinary powers to get things done. Twice he had been disappointed. A third such outcome, he realized, would probably result in his own powers in the theater being circumscribed. Pershing cast about for a man who was relentless, determined, ruthless, and as focused as the job required. His eyes settled on his former chief of staff, General Harbord, who was by this time commanding the Second Division and performing so well that he expected to be promoted to corps command, and perhaps even army command in the near future.

When Pershing called and asked if he would take the job, he must have heard in Harbord's voice his disappointment at the prospect of being taken out of combat command for the tedium of logistics. There was no glory in packing mules with ammo and kicking them down muddy roads. Pershing asked him to sleep on it. But Harbord had once told Pershing that he was his man and could assign him to hell, if he wished. That old loyalty was still there. Crestfallen, Harbord said there was no need to sleep on it. He would take the assignment.

Harbord took charge and improvements were almost immediate. Whereas Blatchford and Kernan rarely left their desks and never visited much of the sprawling rear logistical areas, Harbord put himself on an almost constant inspection tour. To accomplish this, he had a special train car made with sleeping quarters, a kitchen with cook, telegraph, and telephone facilities, and two automobiles for side trips. Harbord cabled Pershing, "The car is comfortable; the cook is good; we do business."

People for whom the commander of the rear zone (now called Services of Supply—SOS) had only been a phantom now saw him on a regular basis. Harbord spent most days on the road, and for fifty-five of his first hundred nights, he slept on his train. He was constantly moving about, asking questions, cutting red tape, and correcting stupidity. Where the stupidity reflected incompetence, heads rolled.[9]

Harbord brought one other crucial quality to the job—his understanding of men. Where Pershing had tried to encourage the men on the docks by promising them a chance in the trenches if they worked hard, Harbord realized that few men welcomed exchanging their current jobs for one that markedly increased their chances of being blown to pieces. Instead, he promised the hardest workers places on the first ships home after the war, and gave them leaves to the Riviera. He also instituted competitions between ports, units, and any other participants he could find. Results were printed in the army newspaper, *Stars & Stripes,* posted in SOS centers, and sent home for publication. The result was intense rivalries in almost every SOS endeavor. The AEF inspector general observed, "In the twinkling of an eye a great change came over the entire SOS. It was as if some great force had suddenly awakened from a slumber."[10]

Of course, considering the size and scope of the endeavor, the storage and movement of supplies was never easy and severe problems existed up to and even after the armistice. Pershing still had to involve himself in fixing the most glaring problems or to periodically rail against the War Department, which never seemed to send him enough of what he most needed. However, in Harbord, Pershing had found his man. Although problems persisted, Pershing never doubted that Harbord was doing everything humanly possible to fix them. As far as Pershing was concerned, if a problem were outside Harbord's ability to solve, it was not solvable by mortal man.

After the establishment of a workable logistics infrastructure and organization, the second great problem was purchasing. On his stopover in Britain, Pershing had learned that the critical issue of the war was shipping. Available shipping was already stretched to near the breaking point, while the U-Boats were sinking ships faster than the Allies could replace them. The belated institution of the convoy system made a major difference, but shipping space remained at a premium until the war's end. To alleviate this burden, it was critical for the AEF to purchase as much materiel as possible in-country. This included everything from French farm produce to artillery and aircraft.

Unfortunately, there was no central purchasing agency for the Allies. In direct competition with the Americans, British and French agents were scouring every factory and business to purchase every extra item available in order to support their own war machines. Pershing convened a committee to study the problem. It concluded that a collective purchasing board would be illegal and recommended that the Americans get out there and compete with the British and French. Pershing considered this method chaotic, so he ripped up the report and went looking for someone who could run American purchasing and coordinate requirements with the Allies. It would take an especially tenacious and assertive man with rare talents in organization and diplomacy.

As Pershing made final preparations to move from Paris to his new headquarters at Chaumont, an old friend dropped in to visit—Charlie Dawes. Dawes, a pal from Pershing's days at the University of Nebraska, was a drinking buddy, a confidant, and one of the smartest and most capable men Pershing knew. Dawes had finagled his way to the European theater as an engineer officer by exaggerating his technical credentials—he once had a summer job where he had held a string for a surveyor. When he volunteered for military service he was already a successful lawyer and politician, and he would one day be vice president of the United States.

Pershing told Dawes that he could do good service in the engineers, but that the AEF could better use his talents with the more important task of coordinating AEF purchasing in Europe. Dawes leapt at the opportunity to do an important job, especially one for which he considered himself uniquely suited. Dawes wrote in his journal:

> [Pershing] gives me practically unlimited discretion and
> authority to go ahead and devise a system of coordination
> of purchases, to arrange the liaison between the French

and English army boards and our own; to use any method which may seem wise to me to secure supplies for the army in Europe. In other words he makes me an important element in the war. I will not fail him.[11]

Based on their long friendship, Dawes had a special relationship with Pershing. He was the only person in the AEF who dared call Pershing by his first name. Staff officers also noted that whenever Dawes was nearby, the general was more relaxed and mirthful. During one luncheon with Pershing and key members of his staff, Dawes swept his hand around the elegant dining room of Ogden Mills' mansion and quipped. "John, when I contrast these barren surroundings to the luxuriousness of our early life in Lincoln, Nebraska, it does seem that a good man has no real chance in the world." Pershing looked around a moment and replied, "Don't it beat hell!"[12]

Some of Pershing's staff were not as confident in Dawes as their boss was. He soon won his critics over, though, when the day after he was appointed to the position, Dawes delved into a coal shortage that was reaching crisis proportions. In short order, he found new sources in England, arranged rail carriage in both England and France, and beat up on War Department bureaucrats to provide the tonnage allotment to move it across the Channel. The dispatch with which he handled a heretofore unsolvable problem silenced skeptics, even though his unmilitary manner ruffled everyone except Pershing. Once, when Pershing entered a staff meeting, the assembled officers, as was customary, stood up and came to attention. Dawes remained seated despite the glares from the other officers. Pershing, bemused, looked at his friend and said, "Charlie, when the commanding general walks into the room it is customary to move your cigar from one side of your mouth to the other." Although he was usually a stickler for rules, Pershing had found a man who could remove a giant burden from his shoulders. For this, he willingly tolerated a certain slackness in military etiquette, though from time to time he sent his aide over to help Dawes properly put on his uniform for important meetings.

Dawes helped relieve some of the stress Pershing was under, but there were needs that even an old drinking buddy could not help him with. Since his early days at West Point, Pershing had enjoyed female companionship. It brought out the flirt in him, and he liked the diversion of social company that allowed him to take his mind off the war. One frequent visitor to his headquarters was Dorothy Canfield Fisher, a student from his Nebraska days and by then a renowned novelist. There is no indication that their relationship ever became intimate, but Pershing greatly enjoyed her social company. The staff, noting that the boss visibly relaxed after spending time with her, began clearing time on his schedule whenever she was in the area. Still, Pershing longed for something more. At one point he considered bringing Nita Patton over, even going so far as to discuss the possibility with her brother George.

In the end, he decided it would not be proper for him to bring his romantic interest to France when he was forbidding every other general officer in the theater from doing so. At least this was the reason he gave to Patton. The reality was that Pershing's romantic interest in Nita had cooled, although he kept that knowledge from everyone, except Nita herself. She had immediately detected it when his letters to her took on a new formality.

The reason for this sudden coolness was Micheline Resco, who would soon become the most important person in Pershing's personal life.[13] Short, blonde, and bright-eyed, Micheline was a Romanian who had become a naturalized French citizen. At twenty-three, she was already recognized as an artistic prodigy, with an easy facility for making friends. Contemporaries described her as very feminine, possessed of a winning laugh, modest, and something of a coquette. In short, she charmed everyone she met. Pershing met her at a Paris reception in mid-June 1917 and though there were some language difficulties, they immensely enjoyed each other's company. By July, three weeks after his arrival in France,

Pershing was writing her affectionate letters. By September they were lovers.

Whenever Pershing visited Paris, he secretly visited her at night, instructing his drivers to remove any emblems that would identify the car. Her apartment became a refuge from the war and, long afterward, she related that Pershing never spoke about the war when he was with her, except once to say, "I feel like I have the weight of the world on my shoulders." Micheline was a discrete woman and satisfied to wait in the shadows for the man with whom, by all accounts, she was deeply in love. They were perfect companions despite the thirty-two-year age difference.

When Pershing left France in 1919, he did not take her with him, even though, judging from their correspondence, his love remained strong. Pershing later had other women in his life, but his passion for Micheline never diminished. After he retired from the army, he spent six months of each year in France overseeing the Battle Monuments Commission, attending receptions, and visiting with Micheline. Throughout their relationship, he sent her a regular monthly check and in 1926 he named her as the beneficiary of his life insurance policy. She was with him in his last days and they secretly married in 1946.

After his death, Pershing's son delivered a letter to Micheline that Pershing had written for this occasion. It began: "What a beautiful love has been ours! How perfect the confidence and the communion! How happy have been the days we have spent together. . . . In all the future the lingering fragrance of your kisses shall be fresh on my lips."[14]

Micheline Resco and the other ladies who visited the headquarters may have been pleasant distractions, but Pershing never allowed himself to be diverted for long. By fall 1917 he had four divisions to train. The First Division, which had been in France since late

June 1917, was joined by the Second Division, consisting of a brigade of soldiers and a brigade of marines; the Twenty-Sixth Division of the New England National Guard; and the Forty-Second Division, called the Rainbow Division, because it was a composite of guardsmen from many states. As with the First Division, many of these unit's soldiers were new recruits. [15]

The AEF followed the Allied system of setting up special training centers and schools to teach subjects such as gas warfare, demolitions, and the use of hand grenades and mortars. Pershing had a problem with the Allies' exclusive emphasis on only training for trench warfare and insisted on additional training in offensive tactics, including detailed work in rifle marksmanship and the use of the bayonet. Ideally, each division would go through their training cycle in three or four months, but conditions were rarely ideal. Soldiers and units arrived from the United States lacking basic skills. Moreover, regimental and divisional officers were often sent away from their units to attend schools, while the enlisted men were called on to perform numerous labor details.[16]

While the units underwent training regimes, Pershing was rating their commanders and future commanders. Secretary Baker had instituted a program, of which Pershing did not entirely approve, to send perspective divisional commanders to Europe for an orientation before their units were even mobilized. Making the best of the distraction, Pershing turned the visits into a combination test and extended job interview. As the generals departed for the United States, some would be given a letter addressed to Baker. On it would be a list of the generals Pershing did not want to see back in France under any circumstances and the reasons why. Sometimes the officer Pershing ordered dispensed with would be the one selected to carry home the letter ending his career.

By the end of 1917, Pershing had removed two of his four division commanders, put the fear of God into the third, and removed the rear area commander, all in his quest for immediate results. To replace General Sibert in the First Division, Pershing selected Major General Robert Lee Bullard, a tough man whom Pershing had known at West Point and in the Philippines. Pershing admired his principles on war-fighting. On taking command, Bullard insisted that his commanders begin to teach their men how to hate, and repeatedly told his men that the division's watchword would be, Kill, Kill, KILL![17]

Interestingly, Bullard did not originally think highly of Pershing. He recalled Pershing's performance in the Philippines and the great lengths he would go to in order to avoid battle. Based on this, he considered Pershing weak and wrote of him, "Pershing is not a fighter; he is in all his history a pacifist and unless driven thereto will do no fighting in France for many a day."[18] When Pershing first told Bullard he was considering replacing Sibert and giving him command of First Division, Sibert confided in his journal, "Gen. Pershing is hardly strong enough to do this. I do not believe he has the force."[19] As Bullard freely admitted later, he had greatly underestimated the will, resolution, and fighting spirit of his commander.

+>===<+

By October, 1917, Pershing was sure enough of the First Division to allow it to go into the trench line in one- and two-battalion rotations for ten days. In its first rotation the American army was bloodied. As soon as the Germans realized there was an untested American unit in front of them, they launched a short, sharp raid to break American morale. At 3:00 A.M., on November 4, the Germans unleashed a heavy box barrage on an isolated outpost of the Sixteenth Infantry Regiment. For over an hour shells rained down, cutting off all communications to the outpost. As soon as the artillery stopped, German raiders, four times the number of the Americans, descended on the outpost from two sides.

For the next quarter of an hour there was a wild melee. Seasoned German veterans rolled in grenades, slashed with trench knives, and fired Lugers at point blank range, while the Americans fought back just as viciously. When it was over, five Americans were wounded, twelve taken prisoner, and three killed: One was shot, one had his throat cut, and the last had his skull bashed in. Even though surprised and outnumbered, the Americans had killed two Germans and wounded seven more. For the first time, American army units were in action and Corporal James Gresham, Private Thomas Enright, and Private Merle Hay became the first American battle deaths of the war.

When Pershing heard the battle reports, he wept.

CHAPTER 10

Into the Fight

NOVEMBER 1917 WAS A DISASTROUS MONTH FOR THE ALLIES.
Russia collapsed into chaos and revolution, releasing dozens of
German divisions for operations on the Western Front. Using the
first seven of these divisions, the Germans spearheaded an Austrian
drive against the Italians at Caporetto that shattered the Italian
army, which retreated over sixty miles before it could make another
stand. What had been a three-front war was now essentially a single
front.[1] Adding to Allied anxieties was another dismal British performance. Haig finally called off his failing Ypres and Passchendaele campaigns, but not before his army had been reduced by a
further 200,000 men from the year before.

The math was not good. According to Pershing's intelligence
section, which even this early in the American involvement was superior to the French and British intelligence staffs, the Germans

would be able to concentrate a formidable force against the Allies in the spring. Germany would be able to muster as many as 217 divisions to face 169 Allied divisions. Since American divisions were double the size of Franco-British units, the Allies would actually have 171 division equivalents, still forty-six less then the Germans.

The French and British were also doing the math, and not liking the looks of things from their perspective. Their regiments and divisions were depleted, and they needed manpower—American manpower. The United States had declared war nine months before, and yet they had only 175,000 soldiers in Europe, many building warehouses or working the docks. When an American truck driver accidentally ran down a Frenchman in Paris, many jeered that the Americans were killing Frenchmen before they killed any Germans.[2]

In December, the Allies once again began a big push for amalgamation. They argued that they had the existing division and corps staff that the Americans had yet to build, and that the war might be lost before America could establish similar organizations. Moreover, amalgamation of U.S. troops into established Allied organizations would solve the shipping problem, as the United States could focus on shipping men only and forget about shipping everything else required to complete a divisional organization. Finally, amalgamation would allow American soldiers to gain real combat experience now, before they were later gathered into an independent American army. Unfortunately, the date for this proposed American army remained nebulous.

Pershing countered, and steadfastly maintained, that national pride demanded there be a separate American army. He maintained that there would be language difficulties serving with the French, while Irish and German Americans would not want to serve with the British. Most important, amalgamation would limit America's role in the postwar peace negotiations. President Wilson certainly would not agree to anything that might reduce his international stature after the war.

Pershing also had more personal objections to amalgamation. Always in the back of his mind was the British and French generals' impressive record of piling up bodies. As Marshal Joffre once commented, it took about 15,000 infantry casualties to train a major general, and Pershing did not want them learning their craft with American blood. Moreover, by this point in the war Lloyd George so distrusted General Haig that he deliberately kept men in England so his generals could not fruitlessly waste what remained of British manhood. And no American politician would survive the outcry if 100,000 American corpses were lying in the mud of Passchendaele because of orders issued by foreign commanders.[3] As far as Pershing was concerned, if Americans were going to die in this war, they would do so only under American commanders and the American flag.

Supported by the president and the secretary of war, Pershing resisted all entreaties. However, this only caused the Allies to redouble their efforts. When presidential advisor Colonel House visited France, Pershing's supposed friend, General Petain, informed House that Pershing was not up to the task. At the same time, French and British generals, ambassadors, and politicians made their way to Washington to argue their case—that Pershing was endangering the entire war effort by resisting amalgamation. Finally, Secretary Baker dispatched the army chief of staff, General Tasker Bliss, to London and Paris as the American representative to the newly established Supreme War Council, to examine the Allied case for amalgamation.

When Bliss arrived in London, he received a briefing on a new proposal to use British ships to transport 150 U.S. infantry battalions. Throughout his stay, he received a continuous stream of important visitors pressuring him to talk sense into Pershing on the amalgamation issue. Bliss reported to Baker, "they all seem very rattled over here. . . . They want men and they want them badly. . . . If we do not make the greatest sacrifices now and, as a result, a great disaster should come, we will never forgive ourselves, nor will the world forgive us."

While the British were making headway with the army chief of staff, Pershing continued to resist. He wanted to know why the British were begging for 150,000 Americans while keeping a million of their own men in England and 1.2 million more in secondary theaters. He also wondered aloud why the British had never offered this apparently excess shipping capacity before. Not convinced of the urgency of amalgamation, Pershing offered a counterproposal: allow the AEF to use the offered tonnage to ship six full divisions rather than 150 battalions.[4] His proposal fell on deaf ears.

When Bliss arrived in France in late January 1918, to participate in the first meeting of the Supreme War Council, Pershing was astonished to discover his old friend agreeing to the Franco-British position in an open meeting, thereby creating an exploitable breach in the solid American wall of resistance to amalgamation. Flabbergasted, Pershing declared himself unalterably opposed to American battalions serving in British divisions. That ended the meeting. That night he went at Bliss with everything he had, until Bliss finally said they should both present their views to Washington and ask for a decision. Pershing retorted, "Well, Bliss, do you know what would happen should we do that? We would both be relieved of further duty in France and that is exactly what we should deserve."[5] Eventually, Bliss came around and promised to support Pershing in the next day's meeting.

The next morning, a succession of British and French generals addressed the meeting and spelled out all of the reasons why amalgamation was critical to Allied survival. Angered but silent, Pershing sat stone-faced through the oratory, but finally exploded at the end. Realizing they had not broken Pershing's resistance, George, still believing the Allies had Bliss in their pocket, asked for the chief of staff's opinion. Bliss looked over the esteemed assemblage and announced, "Pershing will speak for both of us and whatever he says with regard to the disposition of American troops will have my approval."[6] Trapped and once again facing a solid American front, the British caved and agreed to ship over six divisions. However, they did get Pershing to agree that they would be trained behind British lines, in an obvious effort to keep the Americans close enough to grab them at a future date.

+>==>==<+

On March 21, 1918, the long-expected German blow fell upon the British near the Somme. Seventy-one German divisions, under the cover of the largest artillery barrage of the war, smashed into twenty-six weak British divisions. Suddenly a front that had not moved more then ten miles since 1914 had a forty-mile-wide tear in it, and Germans pouring through it. For the first time on the western front the Germans unveiled the tactics that had broken the Russian line at Riga and the Italian line at Caporetto. Popularly called Hutier tactics, for the commander of the German Eighth Army who first employed them at Riga, they were actually first developed and published in a pamphlet by French army captain Andre Laffargue in 1915.[1] This new way of war used a brief but violent bombardment to suppress and shock the front-line soldiers. On the heels of the bombardment came specially trained storm troopers, who were to avoid strong resistance and move quickly into the enemy's rear to disrupt communications, logistics, and the enemy's artillery. Succeeding waves were tasked with reducing bypassed strong-points.

Under this new German blow, the Allies panicked. Petain issued orders for French units to prepare to separate from the British army and cover the approaches to Paris, while Haig began making plans to fall back to the Channel ports and prepare either for a last glorious stand or embarkation to England. Before the Allies finally stopped the Germans just short of their objective at Amiens, the British Fifth Army had suffered 164,000 casualties and lost 90,000 prisoners, 200 tanks, 1,000 guns, and 4,000 machine guns.[7]

While the British Fifth Army was being torn to pieces, its government renewed its push for amalgamation. This time, Secretary

Baker himself was in London and soon found himself being pressed from all sides. Eventually, and with Pershing's concurrence, the Americans agreed that while the British would still ship six full divisions, the priority of shipment would go to machine gun and infantry battalions, at least for the month of May.

Thinking the issue resolved, Pershing went to the May meeting of the Supreme War Council hoping to discuss strategy rather than amalgamation. However, led by French Premier Georges Clemenceau, the Allies launched new broadsides on amalgamation. During the two-day conference, every Allied leader pressed Pershing to bring over American infantry at the expense of the rest of the divisional elements throughout summer 1918. At one point, General Foch asked Pershing in exasperation, "You are willing to risk our being driven back to the Loire?" Pershing replied, "Yes, I am willing to take the risk. Moreover, the time may come when the American army will have to stand the brunt of this war, and it is not wise to fritter away our resources in this manner."[8] Pershing finally brought the first day's meeting to an end by pounding the table and announcing, "Gentlemen, I have thought this program over very deliberately and will not be coerced."[9]

After two days of acrimonious debate, Pershing proposed to continue the agreement to expedite shipping infantry battalions through June, but reserved the decision on continuing such movement into July for the future. The Allies unhappily accepted the new arrangement, in which the British would transport 130,000 Americans in May and 150,000 more in June. American shipping would be used to transport artillery, engineer, and other support and service troops to build a separate American army.

On April 9 the Germans' second great offensive struck another sector of the British front. This time they were aiming for the channel ports, intending to cut the British off from home. On April 11, Haig panicked. He begged the French for help and issued his famous back-to-the-wall order: "Every position must be held to the last man; there must be no retirement. With our backs to the wall, and believing in the justice of our cause, each one of us must fight on to the end. The safety of our homes and the freedom of mankind alike depend upon the conduct of each of us at this critical moment."[10]

Many histories written since the Great War have painted this as a Churchillian speech that rallied the British army to dig in its heels and hold the line. Pershing, however, saw it for what it was: Haig had lost his nerve and was on the verge of defeat. His message was the last bravado of a man at the point of collapse; and Petain, when he and Clemenceau visited with Haig, commented that the British commander was a beaten man who would probably surrender in the field within two weeks. When Pershing first saw the message, he was visiting with General Douglas MacArthur, another former West Point first captain. He read the note to MacArthur and commented, "We old First Captains, Douglas, must never flinch," a pointed comment about Haig, who in Pershing's eyes was clearly flinching.

Earlier, General Foch had asked Pershing what he could do to help during this great crisis. Pershing replied:

> . . . the American people would consider it a great honor for our troops to be engaged in the present battle. I ask you for this in their name and my own.
>
> At the moment there is no other questions but of fighting. Infantry, artillery, aviation, all that we have is yours: use them as you wish. More will come, in numbers equal to the requirements.[11]

It was a grandiloquent boast, but now it was time to deliver. General Bullard and the First Infantry Division withdrew from a quiet sector of the line, where they had been gaining experience, and moved to the aid of the French, near Cantigny. Before they left, Pershing spoke to the division's officers: "You are going to meet an enemy, a savage enemy, flushed with victory. Meet them like

Americans. When you hit, hit hard and don't stop hitting. You don't know the meaning of the word defeat. When you go into battle . . . use your heads and hit the line hard!"

By the time the First Division moved into its positions, the British and French had already broken the back of the German offensive. The Allied front had stretched to the limit of endurance and several times appeared on the verge of destruction. But despite this, it was not a one-sided fight. After the Allies recovered from their initial shock, survivors dug in and fought back with grim determination. By May, German losses went over the six-figure mark and at the same time they began outrunning their logistics. In modern military parlance, the German offensive had reached its "culminating point." It petered out.

+>====<+

It was now the end of May 1918, and the United States had been at war for fourteen months. But its troops had yet to see serious action beyond a few raids and small melees, and in these cases the units involved hardly covered themselves in glory. Pershing decided to use the First Division as a test case of American offensive capability. He ordered it to take the ridge to its front at Cantigny—and hold it. Since 1914, the French had taken and then lost Cantigny twice. Pershing was determined that the First Division would take it once, and hold it.

George C. Marshall meticulously planned the attack, and the regiment selected was heavily reinforced by over 250 heavy French artillery pieces, seventeen French tanks, extra engineers, and a flamethrower platoon. On May 28, following closely behind a rolling artillery barrage, Colonel Ely's Twenty-Eighth Regiment went forward. Although facing approximately an equal number of Germans in two regiments, Ely's men made quick progress. Before dusk, the Twenty-Eighth secured all of its objectives.

Pershing was on hand at First Division headquarters when the attack commenced. His tense demeanor betrayed how much importance he placed on the success of this first American offensive. As reports of complete success came in, Pershing turned to Bullard and with a bit more emotion than he was in the habit of revealing, asked, "Do [the French] patronize you? Do they assume superior airs with you?" Bullard replied, "They do not. . . . I know them too well," and it is hard to imagine anyone condescending to Bullard, who went about his headquarters every day exhorting his men to think about nothing but killing. Pershing, immensely proud of what his men had just accomplished, almost shouted, "By God! They have been trying it with me, and I don't intend to stand for it."[12]

He need not have worried, for Gallic feelings of superiority were at the moment being tested to the First Division's south. Just as the Cantigny assault commenced, the French were confronting their worst crisis since 1914, as Ludendorff launched his third great offensive of 1918. Although there had been plenty of warning from intelligence services (in fact General Nolan's AEF intelligence section had predicted the location and almost the exact time of the attack), the Germans caught the French command by surprise.

To meet the growing emergency, the French withdrew all of their heavy artillery from the Cantigny attack. Ely's men were left to fight off six strong counterattacks without support from any of the big guns that could reach the German artillery. American infantry was left at the mercy of large-caliber German guns, which promptly began to chew them up. The Twenty-Eighth fought with only machine guns, rifles, grenades, and what support General Summerall's small-caliber divisional artillery could provide. At one point, Ely was calling on Summerall's 75 MM guns to break up enemy concentrations so often that he apologized. Summerall replied, "That is what we are here for. We don't criticize and we don't ask questions."

For three days Ely's Twenty-Eighth Regiment beat off everything the Germans could throw at them, yet endured frightful losses from heavy artillery. Worried, Pershing sent an order to Bullard stating that under no circumstances must his division quit the positions they had gained. Because Bullard could not replace the Twenty-Eighth with a fresh regiment while it was under such severe shelling, Pershing's order basically told Ely and his men to hold or die. They held!

When the Sixteenth Regiment finally relieved the Twenty-Eighth Regiment, the latter had suffered over 1,000 casualties, ostensibly to hold an unimportant village that few Americans had ever heard of. But this fight was about more then a patch of land. It was a battle of wills and a first test of strength, and the Americans had won. As George Marshall later said, "The losses we suffered were not justified by the importance of the position itself. However, they were many times justified by the importance of other great and far-reaching considerations."[13]

Pershing was elated by the success. At a dinner party held during the Cantigny battle, Dorothy Canfield Fisher recorded that Pershing listened to his staff talk excitedly about the magnificent conduct of American troops. Then, without warning, he brought his fist down on the table, shouting out, "I am going to jump down the throat of the next person who asks me, will the Americans really fight."[14] The Americans had proven that they could and would fight, and this knowledge had come at a key moment, for the French now needed American help in the worst way.

As Ely's troops were beating off repeated German counterattacks, the French army was disintegrating in the Chemin des Dames area, which until now had been a quiet sector. It was used by both French and German armies as a rest area for divisions broken elsewhere. The Germans even referred to it as the "sanatorium of the west." By May 30, the Germans had ripped a thirty-mile hole in the French line and penetrated thirty miles. As a result, the

French had lost another 100,000 men, while 60,000 more were marched into captivity. It was a rout, and, except for Petain, everyone once again promptly panicked. When Clemenceau sent his chief of staff forward to get a true measure of the situation, he found a corps commander, General Joseph DeGoutte, crying over a tattered map.[15]

As the French army suffered, Pershing had lunch with Haig, who went on at great length about the poor showing the French were making. Privately, Pershing found such criticisms from Haig quite remarkable given the beating the Germans had given him just a few weeks previously, but he refrained from commenting. However, Pershing did learn one important fact from Haig: The British had no combat-ready forces to offer the French in their hour of need.

Pershing left Haig to visit with Allied Supreme Commander General Foch late in the day on May 30. Pershing found him agitated and gloomy about French prospects. Although the fate of France would be decided within the next few days, Foch railed about the necessity of shipping over American infantry for amalgamation into French units—a course of action that, even if Pershing agreed to it, would take months to have a practical effect. Pershing gave him the same time-tested arguments as to why such a decision was not advisable and tried to focus Foch on the immediate problem and on what American troops could do to help. However, Foch seemed unable to focus on the present situation and Pershing eventually gave up.

Pershing was dejected. Foch, the man who never lost his nerve and was almost a caricature of the French offensive sprit, now seemed defeated. If the French could not find a general to take charge, they were doomed. Once again, Petain rose to save France. Alone among the senior French generals, he kept his head and desperately gathered divisions to build a new line. As May ended, Petain urgently requested that Pershing commit American divisions to the battle. When the request arrived, Pershing was locked in another grueling debate over amalgamation with French and British government officials. Proving that he was not inflexible, Pershing agreed to allow American troops to fight under French command, as long as there was a real crisis and the Americans fought as intact divisions.

Within hours after Petain's request, Pershing had his Second and Third Divisions heading into the jaws of the main German thrust. Meanwhile, the First Division, expecting relief at Cantigny, was ordered to stay in the line and expand its front to the north, so that the French could withdraw a division for use elsewhere. To accomplish this expansion, Colonel George Marshall armed two battalions of noncombat support troops and put them into the Cantigny line with a simple order, "You are to die east of the rail line."

As the Second and Third Divisions advanced into the line, they passed through the detritus of a retreating French army. For the first time the Americans were seeing what defeat looked like, as thousands of exhausted, hollow-eyed men, no longer capable of fighting, headed for the rear. To the Americans, they looked terrified.

The Second Division, commanded by Major General Omar Bundy, was a Regular Army division and Pershing himself had selected many of its officers. One of its two brigades was a Marine brigade commanded by Pershing's former chief of staff, Army Brigadier General Harbord. The division was well trained and had been in the trench line for several months before being ordered to the aid of the French. As with the First Division, Pershing had total confidence in the Second Division, although he was mindful that its weak link was its commander.

Bundy was not a strong leader, and Pershing doubted he was forceful enough to resist nonsensical Allied demands or to push his men hard in combat. To compensate, Pershing assigned Colonel Preston Brown as Bundy's chief of staff. Brown was smart, hard working, and mean. He had progressed through the army despite having been accused, but not proven, of having illegally executed insurgents in the Philippines. Brown felt no need to please anyone, much less get along with anyone, and Bundy was often content to let him deal with the Allies and run the Second Division.

As the Americans arrived, the local French commander, General DeGoutte, having pulled himself together since Clemenceau's chief of staff found him crying over a map, ordered the American division committed to the battle as its regiments arrived. This piecemeal emplacement of the arriving regiments would have ensured they were each under the command of a French division, or amalgamated by default. Bundy was against the idea, but said nothing. Preston Brown, however, refused and stated that the Americans would form a new line behind the French, through which they could fall back. DeGoutte eventually agreed and asked the Americans to take a position facing east toward Château-Thierry. Still anxious, DeGoutte turned to Brown and asked, "Can the Americans really hold?" Brown looked up from his map and quietly replied, "General, these are American regulars. In a hundred and fifty years they have never been beaten. They will hold."

The Second Division had little trouble holding. Like most World War I offensives, this one was petering out because the Germans could not bring supplies forward fast enough to sustain forward momentum. Recent histories, particularly those by Europeans, have tended to minimize the contributions of the Second and Third Divisions in stemming the German advance. What they have ignored is that for five days not a single French unit had stood its ground and fought. The only words French soldiers, streaming to the rear, spoke to Americans were, "The war is lost." The Second Division was the first unit to stand, and Foch told Pershing at the time that the Americans had saved Paris. But the Second Division did more than stand. It went forward.[16]

On June 6, Harbord ordered his Marine brigade to attack into Belleau Wood. Famously, a sergeant who had already won two Medals of Honor, Dan Daly, shouted to his men, "Come on, you sons-o-bitches. Do you want to live forever?" as they surged forward. The fight was on and it was to continue for another twenty-one days. It was a brutal battle for a worthless copse, leaving 5,000 Marines dead or wounded. Once again, though, it was not the patch of ground that mattered. It was another test of wills to determine if there was to be a separate American army. General Erich Ludendorff had ordered that, if the Americans were encountered, they were to be given a particularly severe blow to crush their morale and postpone indefinitely their ability to create their own army.

After Harbord's Marines had chewed up two German reserve divisions, Ludendorff sent in two crack first-line divisions, the Tenth and Twenty-Eighth. It made no difference to the outcome, as inch by inch the marines clawed their way through the best the German army had to offer. The commander of the Twenty-Eighth Division put it succinctly, "It is not a question of the possession or nonpossession of this or that village or woods. It is a question whether the Anglo-American claim that the American army is equal or the superior of the German army is to be made good." The answer came on June 26, when the marines sent a message back to headquarters: "This Wood now exclusively U.S. Marine Corps."[17]

Soon after the battle, Pershing visited some of the hospitals. Several Marines stood by their beds at attention and saluted, their sightless eyes heavily bandaged. One Marine apologized for not saluting. Pershing, noting there was no bulge in the sheet where the Marine's right arm should be, replied, "It is I who should salute you." Pershing remained cheerful and upbeat throughout his visit; however, during the drive home tears began to flow. He turned to Dawes, who had accompanied him, and told him that he had great difficulty controlling his emotions when he saw men maimed as a result of his orders. He hoped God would be good to them.[18]

Ludendorff, however, was not yet done. He launched both a fourth and fifth offensive. Intelligence alerted the Allies to the date and location of the fourth offensive and, before the attack, heavy

French artillery smashed up the German assault formations. The fourth offensive ended almost as soon as it had begun. The fifth offensive was more successful and almost broke through to Paris.

At midnight, July 15, the German artillery fire crashed into the Allied lines and the last German push of the war began. As AEF intelligence had predicted, it aimed at breaking through the Marne east of Château-Thierry, where the Third Division had been dug in for six weeks. That night and the next day the Thirty-Eighth Infantry Regiment, Third Division, made a stand that deserves to rank with the most famous last stands in military history, with one difference—it won. Captain Jesse Wooldridge described some of the battle:

> At 3:30 A.M. the general fire ceased and their creeping barrage started—behind which at 40 yards only, mind you, they came—with more machine guns than I thought the German Army owned. . . .
>
> The enemy had to battle their way through the first platoon on the river bank—then they took on the second platoon on the forward edge of the railway where we had a thousand times the best of it—but the [Germans] gradually wiped it out. My third platoon [took] their place in desperate hand to hand fighting, in which some got through only to be picked up by the fourth platoon which was deployed simultaneously with the third. . . . By the time they struck the fourth platoon they were all in and easy prey.
>
> It's God's truth that one Company of American soldiers beat and routed a full regiment of picked shock troops of the German Army. . . . At ten o'clock . . . the Germans were carrying back wounded and dead [from] the river bank and we in our exhaustion let them do it— they carried back all but six hundred which we counted later and fifty-two machine guns. . . . We had started with

251 men and 5 lieutenants. . . . I had left 51 men and 2 second lieutenants.[19]

Before the fighting was done the Thirty-Eighth Infantry Regiment had beaten back two crack German divisions and demolished the Sixth Grenadier Guards so badly that only 150 of its 1,700 men were found alive the next day. A Grenadier survivor recalled:

Never have I seen so many dead men, never such frightful battle scene. The Americans had nerve; we must give them that; but they also displayed a savage roughness.

"The Americans kill everybody!" was the cry of terror of July 15th, which for a long time stuck in the bones of our men.

In eerily similar phraseology, over eighty years later, an Iraqi general captured by the same Third Infantry Division in 2003 stated, "It is impossible to fight the Americans who engage and kill everything and everyone on the battlefield."[20] Success had a heavy price, but the Third Infantry paid it and earned a unit nickname that continues today—"The Rock of the Marne."

Because it presents a startling example of the problems that Pershing foresaw if full amalgamation ever became a reality, there is one last story from this battle that demands telling. To fill a gap in the French line, four rifle companies of the Twenty-Eighth Division from the Pennsylvania National Guard were attached to the French division east of the Thirty-Eighth Infantry. When the French retreated, they neglected to inform the Pennsylvanians, whom the Germans promptly surrounded. Most of them were killed or captured and only a few fought their way south to rejoin their comrades after a harrowing ordeal. Mistakes happen in war, but the odds are considerably increased when language and cultural differences are added to the command mix.[21]

The Allies had stopped Ludendorff, and Pershing immediately began talking to Foch and Clemenceau about launching a counteroffensive. Pershing strongly recommended an attack toward Soissons, which would cut the German supply routes to their troops along the Marne and force them to abandon all of the gains from their last three great offensives. Foch, who had been looking for a place to strike a counterblow, assented.

By the end of June, five American divisions were positioned in the Château-Thierry area. Pershing decided to use this concentration for the first tactical employment of an AEF corps headquarters. In mid-June, Pershing ordered General Hunter Liggett and his previously assembled I Corps headquarters to move to the Château-Thierry region and take command of the American divisions in the area. Liggett and his I Corps staff arrived at Château-Thierry, on June 21. There, I Corps assumed control over the First, Second Third, Fourth, and Twenty-Eighth Divisions. More important, the corps began joint planning with the French III Corps with the object of relieving that corps in place. Two weeks later, I Corps took tactical control of the sector. It was Independence Day, July 4, 1918, and Pershing finally had a corps controlling its own sector of the front. When he had two corps, he would be ready to create an army headquarters to command them.

Fourteen days after I Corps assumed tactical control of its sector it provided the pivot for the first large-scale Allied counteroffensive of 1918. Unfortunately, because the corps arrived late, the First and Second Divisions were reassigned to the French XX Corps for the attack (along with the elite First Moroccan Division, which included the French Foreign Legion). As the attack date neared, Pershing allowed that command arrangement to stand.

The First and Second Divisions spearheaded the Allied attack into the northern face of the Marne salient, toward the high ground south of Soissons to cut key rail supply lines. The First

Division commander, Major General Charles Summerall, who had replaced General Bullard when he received a corps command, was on the left, while General Harbord, who had replaced General Bundy in the Second Division, was on the right. The Moroccan First Division was in the center. Both divisions, after a harrowing approach march, got into position just in time. In fact, the lead battalion of the Second Division had to double time the last mile to the jump-off point and arrived only seconds before the start of the attack. Both commanders made their arrangements in the dark and throughout most of the night neither had the slightest idea where most of their units were, except that they were snarled somewhere in one of the Great War's many massive traffic jams.

Despite the lack of preparation and the confusion, the attack went forward. Both divisions made remarkable progress and by early morning they had advanced over three miles and captured all of their assigned objectives. However, heavy German reinforcements were arriving and, although American infantry inched forward all of July 19, each yard became progressively more costly. After two days of hard fighting, Harbord asked that the Second Division be relieved. In those two days the division had advanced more than eight miles and captured 3,000 prisoners and sixty-six field guns, at a cost of almost 4,000 casualties.[22]

Summerall's division remained in line for another three days. The division had taken heavy losses, but when a concerned French staff officer asked if his division was capable of continuing the attack, Summerall replied, "Sir, when the 1st Division has only two men left, they will be echeloned in depth and attacking towards Berlin." Pershing, who was always on the lookout for aggressive commanders with the will to carry an assault forward, was more than pleased with Summerall, particularly when he heard of Summerall's response to a battalion commander who sent back a report stating he had been stopped by enemy action. Summerall replied, "You may have paused for reorganization, but if you ever send me a message with the word stopped in it again you will be relieved of command."[23]

Before it pulled out of the line, the First Division had cut the Soissons–Château-Thierry highway and the Villers-Cotterêts railroad. In its five-day advance the First Division had fought seven German divisions, and captured 3,800 prisoners and 70 guns. Success had not come cheap. Seven thousand American soldiers had fallen, including three-quarters of the division's field grade officers.[24]

Pershing was ecstatic at the success of his two divisions. When he visited Harbord, he told him, "even if neither the 1st and 2nd Divisions should never fire another shot, they had made themselves and their commanders immortal."[25] Because of the success of the Franco-American attack, the Germans were forced to evacuate the Marne salient and give up all of the gains they had made in their fifth great 1918 offensive. It was the turn of the tide.

From this point forward, the Germans were never able to launch another major offensive. They even had to cancel a planned attack against the British in Flanders, so that divisions could be rushed south to stop the rapidly advancing Americans. Although Ludendorff had come close to shattering the Allied armies in the spring and summer of 1918, in the end he failed. The result was a strategic disaster for the Germans. They had not been able to capitalize on driving Russia out of the war, and by the end of July they had used up their strategic reserve. In late March 1918, the German army in the west held about 330 miles of front; by July that front had been extended to 450 miles. However, in the intervening period their army lost over a million men, with a large share of them coming from crack storm trooper units.[26] As German Chancellor Georg von Hertling later said: "We expected great events in Paris for the end of July. That was on the 15th. On the 18th even the most optimistic among us understood that all was lost. The history of the world was played out in three days."[27]

Pershing knew that in no small measure victory was due to the hard fighting of American soldiers. They had plugged the holes, stopped German stormtroopers dead in their tracks, and then smoothly transitioned into an offensive that swept back what until then was an invincible German tide. They had not done it alone, but by the middle of 1918 it was widely recognized that French units, still shaky from their 1917 mutiny, would not attack unless the Americans went with them.

It would be impossible to underestimate the continuing morale boost the Allies, military and civilian alike, were still getting from the Americans' arrival on French battlefields. Vera Brittain, a British nurse, captured the emotions of many the first time she saw American troops heading into combat: "They looked like Tommies in heaven. I pressed forward to watch the United States physically entering the War, so god-like, so magnificent, so splendidly unimpaired in comparison with the tired, nerve-racked men of the British Army."[28]

Pershing now had 1.2 million American men in Europe, with an average of almost 10,000 more pouring in every day. By the end of August, the United States would have as many men in France as Britain did, and almost as many men in uniform as the French themselves. Despite a continuing logistical nightmare, insufficiently trained staff, and severe shortages of many of the items required for waging modern war, the time for an American army had arrived. Ignoring new amalgamation proposals, such as placing 100 American regiments in Allied divisions and even a plea from the King of England that divisions training behind the British army continue to serve in that sector, Pershing ordered an American army into being. On July 14, 1918, he issued a formal order to form the American First Army, to become effective on August 10. All that was required was to decide which sector the First Army would occupy. Pershing was tempted to ask for the area around the Marne salient, since he had concentrated so many divisions there to help stop Ludendorff's fifth offensive. However, Foch wanted the German salient at St. Mihiel eliminated and Pershing wanted to prove the effectiveness of the American army. After Pershing consulted with Petain, they went to Foch to demand that the American army participate in the reduction of St. Mihiel. This sector also possessed the inestimable advantage of being much closer to the logistical base the AEF had been installing for the past year.

The First Army went into the line around St. Mihiel and started preparations for a major attack. Its objective was to eliminate a position which had successfully resisted several major French attacks since 1914. On August 30, Pershing took direct command of the sector and welcomed Foch to his headquarters.

CHAPTER 11

The First Great Offensive

ON AUGUST 30, 1918, FOCH WALKED INTO PERSHING'S headquarters at Ligny-en-Barrios and promptly attempted to overturn Pershing's planning and undo the progress he had made toward forming an independent American army. Until that moment, Allied attacks had aimed at eliminating the salients created during the Ludendorff offensives. These attacks pushed the Germans back, opened logistics routes, and shortened the front, but they were not yet doing anything decisive to win the war. Foch noticed that the entire German front, as it pushed into France, was one giant salient from the North Sea to Verdun. His idea was to attack the salient like any other, by holding in front and pushing in hard on the shoulders. He planned for the British to intensify their already ongoing attacks around Amiens and the Somme, and for the French and Americans to hit the northern face of the German lines from the direction of Mézières.

As a first step, Foch told Pershing that the Americans would have to limit or cancel their attack on St. Mihiel. Worse, he wanted Pershing to transfer a number of his divisions to the French Second Army, while at the same time moving the American First Army north to the Argonne area. Moreover, Foch wanted the First Army to attack in two widely separated parts, with the French Fourth Army in between. He also proposed giving the French Fourth Army operational control of the American First Army. Pershing did not miss the point. Foch's conception of future operations had no role for Pershing in command of a separate American army. Possibly unknowingly, Foch added insult to injury by offering to supply a French general to each American division and corps to "assist" in the conduct of operations. After seeing the anger beginning to flare in Pershing's demeanor, Foch said, "I realize I am presenting you with a number of new ideas and you probably need time to think them over, but I should like your impressions."

Pershing required no time. "Marshal Foch," he said, "here on the very day that you turn over a sector to the American army and almost on the eve of an offensive, you ask me to reduce the operation so that you can take away several of my divisions and assign some of them to the French Second Army and use others to form an American army to operate on the Aisne in conjunction with the French Fourth Army, leaving me with little to do except hold a quiet sector. . . . This virtually destroys the American Army that we have been trying so long to form."

Foch said he regretted it, but he saw no other way. As for Pershing, he could clearly see that Foch was trying to place French commanders inside of American units, fragment Pershing's newly assembled army, and ensure that no matter how splendidly American units performed, the French would receive all of the credit. After some discussion, Pershing offered to relieve several French Second Army divisions of their sectors so an American army could concentrate on a single front, under his command. Foch dismissed the proposal and sarcastically countered, "Do you wish to take part in the battle?"

Pershing became angry now: "Most assuredly, but as an American Army and in no other way." Foch replied, "There is no time to send an entire Army." Pershing countered, "Give me a sector and I will occupy it immediately . . . wherever you say."

Disingenuously, Foch referred to the American army's lack of artillery and auxiliary troops. Pershing now became livid and forcefully reminded Foch that it had been the French and British who had for the last several months begged the American government to send over nothing but infantry and machine gun units to help meet the summer crisis and that he, Foch, had personally promised to make up deficiencies in the American organization out of Allied resources. Pershing had foreseen Foch's line of argument when he originally resisted Allied pleas not to waste shipping space on the equipment and auxiliary units required to build up a self-sufficient American force, but that did not lessen his anger.

Foch continued to push his plan, pleading a lack of time to anything that Pershing was offering, as a compromise. Finally Foch appealed to Pershing's soldierly pride: "Your French and English comrades are going into battle; are you coming with them?" Pershing exploded, "Marshal Foch, you have no authority as Allied commander-in-chief to call upon me to yield up my command of the American Army and have it scattered among the Allied forces where it will not be an American Army at all."

"I must insist upon that arrangement," Foch countered.

"Marshal Foch you may insist all you please, but I decline absolutely to agree to your plan. While our army will fight wherever you may decide, it will not fight except as an independent American army!"

Foch was shaken and pale. He handed Pershing a memorandum of his proposal and retreated from the room. He paused at the door and said, "Once you have thought more about it I am sure you will consent."[1]

Like so many before him, Foch had misjudged Pershing. That night, Pershing confided in his diary: "Firmly convinced that it is the fixed purpose of the French, and perhaps the British, that the formation of an American Army should be prevented if possible. Perhaps they do not want America to find out her strength."

The next day, after consulting his staff, Pershing wrote a formal reply to Foch, refusing the offer. He then went to visit Petain in order to enlist his support. Finding Petain in agreement with his plans, both men went to see Foch. Pershing now advocated that he expand his sector from St. Mihiel toward the west, which would allow him to concentrate the entire American force between the Meuse River and the Argonne Forest. He would then be able to attack northwest toward Mézières as Foch wanted, but he would do it as an American army. However, because the American army had concentrated sixty miles away at St. Mihiel, Pershing doubted it could move north in time to meet Foch's schedule. Pershing, therefore, wanted to move the attack date from the fifteenth to the twentieth. Foch, pressed by both senior American and French commanders, agreed to Pershing's proposal, but did not want the large American army sitting idle as the French and British launched their offensives. He asked Pershing if it would be possible to eliminate the St. Mihiel salient without becoming too engaged and then conduct a larger attack on September 25.

It was a seemingly impossible task, but Pershing agreed.

Within the space of two weeks, an untested and barely trained army was undertaking to engage in a massive offensive, disengage itself while under fire, move sixty miles north, and immediately launch another offensive. Tested Franco-British staffs required months to plan a single major offensive, but Pershing was asking his newly formed First Army staff to plan and then conduct two widely separated major attacks in less than three weeks.[2] Pershing later wrote: "It was only my absolute faith in the energy and resourcefulness of our officers of both staff and line and the resolute and aggressive courage of our soldiers that permitted me to accept such a prodigious undertaking."[3] It helped that the First Army operations officer was a planning and organizational genius—Colonel George C. Marshall.

It was no mean task. Pershing had begun concentrating troops for the St. Mihiel offensive in early August. By the time it kicked off, he had 550,000 Americans and 110,00 Frenchmen in position. To support them, he had positioned 3,010 guns, 40,000 tons of ammunition, and an air force, under Colonel Billy Mitchell, of 1,400 planes (none of them American built). He also had a tank brigade of 267 light tanks commanded by his former aide, Lieutenant Colonel George S. Patton.[4]

At 1:00 A.M. on September 12, over three thousand guns belched simultaneously. For the next four hours the guns pounded German positions, road intersections, supply dumps, and artillery positions. It was not the most effective fire of the war, but it encouraged the green American troops and broke the spirit of many German defenders. Overhead, Billy Mitchell's 1,400 planes massed. He had guaranteed Pershing that he would command the air for three days, and he was as a good as his word.

The Germans caught in this hurricane of fire and steel were mostly second-rate divisions, and even before the American attack they were in the process of withdrawing from the salient. Again, many recent historians have used this fact to belittle the American achievement, one even going so far as to claim the battle was "one where the Americans relieved the Germans."[5] This view overlooks the 7,000 American casualties suffered in three days, a testament to the fact that the Germans were not a beaten force. While they may not have been the elite of the German army, and there may have been a number of them ready to surrender, the overriding fact is that most of the Germans in the salient fought and they fought well. Moreover, these troops had been fortifying their positions since they fought off two French offensives in 1915. Barbed wire entanglements, often thirty feet wide, surrounded their line, and tens of thousands of booby-traps had been emplaced. This whole defensive scheme was covered by several thousand machine guns, with interlocked fields of fire.

The offensive represented the coming of age of the American army. Pershing was fighting the first "joint" battle in American history. In this complicated process, his troops were going forward with strong air support, comprised of different wings providing observation for the artillery, support for the infantry, interdiction missions, and long-range bombing, while continuously fighting swirling air battles to keep German aircraft from bombing American soldiers on the ground. Simultaneously, Pershing was fighting a combined-arms fight—the Americans were finally mastering the use of artillery, infantry, and tanks as a concerted team. In its totality, Pershing presented the Germans with something they had not seen from the Allies prior to 1918 and definitely did not expect from the Americans. In the end, it was the synergistic effects of this joint and well-coordinated combined-arms attack that overwhelmed the German defenders. While the Germans may have been in the process of retreating from the salient, they definitely never planned to lose over 10,000 men along with 450 guns and 16,000 prisoners in the process.

The Allied leadership, most of whom doubted that the American attack would succeed, saw the attack for what it was—validation of Pershing's insistence on a separate American army. There would never again be any questions about the competence of American staffs to plan and coordinate a major battle or of any American combat unit's ability to fight one. For the first time, Pershing had commanders in whom he had complete confidence. In the main, they were men in the Pershing mold—fearless, hard-driving men who would stop at nothing to reach their objectives. This was not only true of Pershing-selected division and corps commanders, but also permeated through the ranks. A few of the better known examples include:

- Lieutenant Colonel Wild Bill Donovan, who won the Medal of Honor while leading his men forward yelling, "What do you think this is, a wake?" He would later form the Office of Strategic Services (the forerunner of the CIA) in World War II.
- Major Terry de la Mesa Allen, a brilliant commander of the First Division in World War II, who, after being shot in the mouth, blood streaming down his face, continued to fight and wiped out a machinegun nest before dropping from loss of blood.
- Seargent Harry J. Adams, who captured 300 shell-shocked Germans with an empty pistol.

American commanders had learned the most important element of combat leadership; they must not only be brave, but they must also be *seen* to be brave. This is something the British army, with its strong concepts of honor and class, had known for a long time. As the probably apocryphal story recounts, a new British recruit inquired of his sergeant major where the officers were. "Don't worry," he was told. "They'll be here when it is time to die." But American officers were different. They were not only seen to be brave when it was time to go over the top and "die well." They were brave all the time. Following Pershing's example of visiting his front-line commanders as often as possible, even the most senior American officers were almost always to be found among their men. In fact, visiting British officers often chided their American compatriots about spending too much time with the men and letting them become too familiar.

Not that every commander, however, had yet met Pershing's exacting standards. In his memoirs, he tells of meeting an unnamed division commander and asking him about the condition of his division. The general replied that the men were tired. After reflecting that the division had not been in the line for long and had no reason to be tired, Pershing decided that it was the division commander who was tired. Pershing promptly relieved the commander in favor of a man Pershing considered, "tireless and efficient."[6]

After the battle, Pershing was amused at the findings of a French commission assigned to discover how the Americans had negotiated German barbed wire entanglements so rapidly and efficiently. After much serious study and consideration, the French decided that the Americans had a decisive advantage over the French in crossing barbed wire because of their "long legs and big feet." In reality, the American success at getting past the wire was thanks to special teams of engineers trained for that specific duty, the use of chicken-wire placed on top of the barbed wire to form a bridge, and the willingness of untold hundreds of soldiers to heave themselves on the wire and let their comrades run over them.

With St. Mihiel behind him, Pershing turned to the Meuse-Argonne. In many ways, he would now fight a battle as horrific as Grant had fought in the Northern Virginia Campaign of 1864. But the Meuse-Argonne was made all the more horrible by the technological ingenuity of man, who in the intervening decades had made the battlefield deadlier by several orders of magnitude.

CHAPTER 12

The Meuse-Argonne Offensive

THE FIGHT AT ST. MIHIEL HAD NOT YET ENDED WHEN Pershing started moving the First Army north. It was a complex and difficult task that would have challenged the most experienced staff. There were only three roads into the area, and the First Army would have to share them with the French Second Army, which was vacating. In total, two corps, consisting of eleven divisions, were moving out, while three corps, consisting of fifteen divisions, were moving in. Considering that a single division took up twenty miles of road space, this represented a formidable task. As the divisions moved forward, the rear area troops constructed eighty massive supply depots, erected forty-four hospitals, extended rail lines, emplaced artillery, and built aerodromes. All had to be planned and executed by a staff still managing offensive operations at St. Mihiel.

Twenty-six years later, in what historian Alan Axelrod called his "defining moment," Pershing's former aide, George S. Patton, cemented his legendary status as a great field commander by turning a corps of his Third Army north and riding to the rescue of the 101st Airborne Division at Bastogne during the Battle of the Bulge.[1] Patton's achievement was superb, but it pales in comparison to what Pershing's First Army was to accomplish. In mid-September 1918, in doing the almost impossible, Pershing was ably assisted by the later "architect of victory" of World War II, George C. Marshall, who during this period earned his nickname "the wizard." However, even the wizard was almost humbled by the task, as units moved late or got lost, exhausted horses died in their tracks, vehicles broke down, and promised Allied support never materialized. To make it all work, Pershing unleashed a blizzard of staff officers on the moving units. Like locusts, this mass of young officers swarmed along the approach routes, cajoling, threatening, cursing, and generally making themselves hated by line officers and troops. They had only one purpose, and that was to give Pershing the results he demanded. They delivered. Every element of the army reached its assigned attack location on its scheduled arrival date. It was easily the greatest staff achievement of the war, and further evidence that those officers with long service in France had learned their business.

Unfortunately, Pershing did not have staff with this level of experience elsewhere in the army. The First Army "war horses," the experienced First, Second, Twenty-Sixth, and Forty-Second Divisions, remained at St. Mihiel and were not available for the start of the Meuse-Argonne assault. Of the nine divisions Pershing placed in the line at the start of the attack, only four had seen combat. Two of the remaining five had been in France less than two months and had never even had a rotation into a quiet sector. Even the experienced divisions were filled with new recruits. For example, the Seventy-Seventh Division received 4,000 new soldiers on the eve of the attack, almost all of whom had been in the army a mere six weeks. Most had spent that time traveling to the front. A significant percentage of these new men had never handled a rifle before entering into combat.

What these soldiers did have, however, was optimism and an unconquerable spirit, and, as Pershing knew, in war that counts for a great deal. When a number of these new recruits were encircled and trapped behind German lines, they fought like lions. The famous "lost battalion," commanded by Major Charles White Whittlesey, had pushed deep into the Argonne Forest, expecting French units on their right to advance beside them. Unknown to Whittlesey, the French attack had stalled and his men were soon surrounded by counterattacking Germans. Digging in, the "lost battalion" fought off repeated German assaults even as ammo and food ran low. Whittlesey's soldiers had to crawl under fire to a stream for drinking water. When the unit was rescued six days later, only 194 of its original 550 men remained unscathed. Lack of training was a severe handicap for many of the units in the Argonne, but there is no doubt that the "no quarter" attitude of the average soldier made up for a lot of deficiencies.

Ever since 1918, there has been a long debate over how many Americans were killed needlessly because they went into combat under a doctrine that was not applicable to the situation they confronted and without proper training. The doctrine part of this debate is nonsensical and rests on Pershing's often quoted desire to never lose sight of the importance of "open warfare." As we saw in the training of the 165th Infantry Regiment and demonstrated time and again in the Meuse-Argonne battles, commanders were able to take the best of "open warfare" doctrine and combine it with the requirements of trench warfare to create a winning method. Those who still claim that Pershing should have waited longer to ensure that his new divisions trained properly tend to neglect the daily realities Pershing faced. What would have happened to the Allied attacks in 1918 if the American army had not been present on the front to grind three dozen first-rate German divisions almost out of existence? How many more Americans would have died, if the Germans had been able to regroup after their 1918 losses and meet the Allies in 1919 with refreshed formations? How would the Alliance have held together, if the Americans went another full year before making a major appearance at the front?

Commanders can always find reasons not to attack. Military history is replete with stories of commanders who took counsel of their fears, most notoriously General George McClellan, of whom Lincoln once inquired, "General McClellan, if you are not going to use the Army, do you mind if I borrow it?" Pershing was no Mc-Clellan. Like many commanders before and since he had to engage the enemy with the army he had, not the army he wished he had. The time to attack was 1918, and he went forward with every bit of power he could scrape up.

Lack of experience was not the only problem confronting the First Army. The French had called away their air formations to support their own attacks. As a result, for support in the Meuse-Argonne offensive, Colonel Billy Mitchell could only put half of the aircraft as had flown over St. Mihiel. Moreover, Pershing, who thought he was critically short of tanks when he possessed 272 at St. Mihiel, now had to make do with less than 200.[2] And, though he would eventually have over 4,000 guns supporting the attack—none of them U.S. made—over half were manned by Frenchmen, and many of his new divisions had never trained with their organic artillery units.

Even that does not tell the whole dismal story. Most of the assaulting divisions had never had an aero squadron assigned to them, and few had ever had a gas or a flame company, specialist engineers, or tanks attached. The detailed coordination between parent and attached units is complex, and few of the attacking divisions' staffs knew how to integrate the many pieces of a modern army into a coherent force capable of conducting successful operations against a well-prepared, motivated, and experienced enemy.[3]

On paper, the First Army seemed to have everything stacked against them. However, the Americans were not completely helpless, and did possess some intangible advantages of considerable value. First, it possessed a cadre of handpicked, youthful, trained, confident, and aggressive generals. Moreover, at First Army headquarters Pershing had built a highly competent and efficient staff. What motivated Pershing and his generals was a deep desire to prove to the world that the American officer corps was the equal of any. This was not an army that ran on sentiment. It was goal-driven and determined to achieve any objective set for it. On the darker side, this could very well produce a ruthlessness to get the job done at any cost.[4]

To fight its way through the Argonne, the First Army would require every bit of aggressiveness and ruthlessness that Pershing and his generals could muster. To say the terrain was highly defensible is to grossly understate the situation. It was what General Hunter Liggett called, "A natural fortress beside which the Virginia Wilderness in which Grant had fought was a park." Pershing's chief of staff, Hugh Drum, called it the "most ideal defensive terrain he had ever seen." Pershing would have to drive his forces through what amounted to a twenty-mile-wide tunnel bordered on one side by the Meuse River and on the other by the nearly impenetrable Argonne Forest. In the center of this passage was Montfaucon Hill, which dominated almost the entire sector. Adding to this horror were the Heights of the Meuse to the east and Argonne Hill to the west. Both overlooked the area and could bring a terrible enfilade fire on the American advance.[5]

Nature was only the first of Pershing's problems. For four years the Germans had unremittingly toiled to emplace every defense they could think of: Trench lines were fortified and flanking trenches dug, concrete dugouts were emplaced along with fortified strong points and a seemingly endless number of concrete machine gun bunkers. Swirling through this were hundreds of miles of thick barbed wire, most of it overgrown with vegetation, rendering the wire invisible until soldiers ran into it. Inside of this fortress zone, the Germans had prepared three strong defensive lines, fittingly named after the three Wagnerian witches: Giselher, Kriemhilde, and Freya.[6] Defending these positions were an estimated five German divisions between the Meuse and the Argonne. Even more worryingly, the Germans had the ability to reinforce the area with seven more divisions within seventy-two hours and fifteen divisions within a week. Unfortunately for Pershing, the Germans surmised that something was up before the American attack began. Reinforcements were already pouring into the area.

Against these imposing obstacles, the First Army mustered over 600,000 men, who would attack in three corps consisting of nine divisions on line with another five in reserve. Bullard's III Corps would attack on the east with its right flank resting on the Meuse River, while Liggett's I Corps was to attack on the west, through the Argonne Forest. Inexplicably, Pershing placed the V Corps in the center. Although its commander, General George Cameron, was an experienced division commander, his corps consisted of Pershing's three most inexperienced divisions.

Pershing and his staff envisioned the offensive in two stages. During the first stage, U.S. forces would penetrate through the three German lines, advancing about ten miles and clearing the Argonne Forest to link up with the French Fourth Army at Grandpré. The second stage would consist of a further ten-mile drive to outflank the enemy positions along the Aisne River and prepare for further attacks toward Sedan and Mézières on the Meuse River. Additional operations were planned to clear the heights along the east bank of the Meuse.

━━◆━◆━━

After a three-hour artillery bombardment, at 5:30 A.M. on September 26, 1918, all three corps attacked. Despite a heavy fog, the rugged terrain, and the network of barbed wire, the weight of the American onslaught quickly overran the German forward positions. On both flanks the corps made good progress. In Bullard's III Corps sector, Major General John Hines' Fourth Division advanced nearly four miles, penetrated the German second line, and smashed several counterattacks in the process. On the western flank, Liggett's corps reached its objectives, advancing three miles on the open ground to the east of the Argonne. In the center, however, the Germans checked V Corps south of Montfaucon. It was not until the next day that Cameron's men were able to seize the position.

Throughout the first day's fighting, Pershing remained in his headquarters fretting as patchy reports came in. Despite some good news, Pershing sensed confusion in the V Corps and its divisions. In his diary he confided, "they were new, their staffs did not particularly work well, and they presented the failings of green troops." By nightfall the Americans were meeting stiffened resistance as they came up against the first of the three main defensive lines. In the course of a single day, the Meuse-Argonne Campaign "turned from a sprint to a slugging match."[7]

By September 28, there was no doubt that things were going poorly. Pershing was sufficiently concerned to spend the better part of the day visiting his three corps commanders and several of his division commanders. After the visits he wrote, "I certainly have done all in my power to instill an aggressive spirit into the corps headquarters." That may have been true, but the next morning the Germans gave the Americans a stiff lesson in warfare. They subjected the Thirty-Fifth Division, which was skirting the Argonne Forest, to a fierce counterattack, which stampeded it to the rear. By the end of the day the division had lost hundreds of officers and thousands of men. The Thirty-Fifth Division was an extreme case, but it was an example of the pummeling American divisions were taking all along the line. A tenacious German defense had checked all forward progress.[8]

It was at this time that Clemenceau's chief of staff visited Pershing's headquarters. His later reflections show that he felt the Americans were being taught a much needed lesson:

> I could read clearly in his eyes that, at that moment, he realized his mistake. His soldiers were dying bravely, but they were not advancing, or very little, and their losses were heavy. All that great body of men which the American Army represented was literally struck with paralysis because the brain didn't exist, because the generals and their staffs lacked experience. With enemies like the Germans, this kind of war couldn't be improvised.[9]

Clemenceau himself visited the next day. In his memoirs, Pershing indicates that the premier declared himself pleased with the AEF's progress, but was disappointed that traffic jams kept him from visiting the front. Pershing was either not telling the whole truth about his meeting with Clemenceau or he had disastrously misread the man's impressions of him and his army. The hopeless congestion behind the front was the only thing that made an impression on Clemenceau, and it was a negative one. As a result of this trip, he decided that neither the American First Army nor Pershing were capable of planning or conducting a large-scale offensive. It was an impression that almost had fatal career consequences for Pershing.

Unit losses and tactical confusion forced Pershing to pause the offensive to reorganize and move up supplies. Clemenceau seized on this apparent American failure to push Foch, in his position as the Generalissimo of all the Armies, to relieve Pershing of command and replace him with a qualified French general. At the same time, British and French ambassadors and generals in Washington were told to constantly remind anyone who would listen, particularly the president and secretary of war, that the Allies did not think Pershing was up to the task of conducting a major operation. The president, however, turned a deaf ear, and Secretary Baker was in France and could see for himself what Pershing was up against and what he was doing to overcome his present difficulties.

Foch, on the other hand, took Clemenceau's comments to heart and though he demurred for the moment from relieving Pershing, he did accept the idea that Pershing was not up to the task of commanding an army in combat. Obviously, French and British generals had no trouble forgetting the millions of corpses credited to their own ledgers when they criticized Pershing and other American officers. On October 1, Foch sent General Weygand to Pershing's headquarters with new orders. Foch wanted to insert the French Fourth Army into the center of the American line, which would create excess American divisions in the Argonne region. These he wanted to siphon off for use elsewhere. Foch's message indicated that he wanted two or three divisions for each of the French corps in the area.

The plan made little tactical sense and Pershing saw it for what it was, another attempt to neuter him and break up the American army. The American commander furiously refused, and, faced with such intransigence, Foch withdrew the order. In his memoirs, Pershing claimed he sensed the hand of Clemenceau behind Foch's order and knew that this was not the end of the matter.

He was right. A little over a week later, when the renewed American assault on the Argonne again appeared stymied, Foch once more sent General Weygand with an order for Pershing. Considering the audacity of this order, it is surprising that Pershing makes no mention of it in his memoirs. It probably still rankled him over a decade later and, rather than show his anger, he decided it was best to omit the entire event from his personal record. This new order relieved Pershing of command of the First Army and placed General Andre Hirschauer, currently commanding the French Second Army, in command. Foch ordered Pershing reassigned to a quiet sector where he would not be troubled with traffic problems or combat. It is astonishing that, after all his prior dealings with Pershing, Foch could consider this a realistic order. When Weygand's aide showed a copy of the order to Pershing's French aide, he was incredulous. "It will never be obeyed," he stated flatly, and could only imagine the horrors Weygand was being subjected to in Pershing's inner office.

The meeting ended abruptly and a clearly flustered Weygand beat a hasty retreat from Pershing's office. As he left the American headquarters he cabled Foch that "he was coming home," and asked Pershing's aide if he saw the order. The aide told him he had, and Weygand shouted "It's all off" before storming from the office. It was not over for Pershing, however, and the next day he went to confront Foch in his headquarters. Foch, reading Pershing's mood, avoided the question of the relief order and instead asked for a briefing on the First Army's fight.

After listening to the short briefing, Foch was not impressed. He commented that the American army was not giving him the results he demanded and was not up to the same standards of the French or British forces. Pershing did little to check his anger and in no uncertain terms told the generalissimo that no army could do any better, given the conditions his soldiers confronted. After a chilly discussion, Weygand intervened and informed Foch that Pershing had brought with him a new plan for the Argonne and a proposal to create another American army so that he could step up to the role of American supreme commander and leave many of the details that were overburdening him to his army staffs.

Foch, probably seeking an escape from the increasingly unpleasant conversation, took the opportunity to change topics, although the air remained frosty. Pershing had gained one precious result from the stormy meeting, however. His proposal to create another American army ended all serious discussions of subjects that had plagued him since he had arrived in Europe: amalgamation, the breaking up of the American army, and a reduction of his responsibilities. He was free to concentrate his energies on winning the war.

Unfortunately, at that moment Pershing was not winning. The first renewed American assaults had made progress on the first day, but then became bogged down in a welter of blood and destruction. After only a few days Pershing was forced to allow his corps commanders to halt and reorganize. Understanding that the center sector was still the campaign's center of gravity, Pershing pulled the four inexperienced divisions assigned to that sector out of the line. In their place went the veteran First, Thirty-Second, and Third Divisions. By October 4, the First Army was ready to attack again.

Unfortunately, the Germans had made good use of the pause. Fresh, veteran, first-rate divisions went into the line facing the Americans. The American attacks went forward fearlessly, often ferociously, but they met hard troops in well-prepared positions. Americans died by the thousands as they fought for every yard against "one damned machinegun after another."[10] But they crawled forward, and by October 10 Liggett's I Corps had cleared the Argonne, while the other corps were finally bashing against the main German defensive belt, the Kriemhilde Stellung. However, nowhere along the line were the Germans cracking. By October 12 the First Army was a spent force.

To keep the attack going as long as it had, Pershing was forced to cannibalize two recently arrived divisions to replace the 80,000 men his front line divisions had lost. Manpower, however, was just one of the problems besetting the Americans. Despite the almost superhuman efforts of his rear area commander, Harbord, U.S. logistical operations were on the verge of collapse. The AEF was short 100,000 horses, and of the 30,000 Harbord was requesting from America each month, less than a thousand were arriving. Trucks, always in short supply, were now critically short, and with the French attacking all along their line, they had no vehicles left to lend to the AEF. Several of Pershing's divisions were immobilized due to lack of transport, and only by the most heroic efforts was it possible to get enough food and ammunition forward to sustain even the feeblest operations.

Adding to Pershing's problems was the outbreak of the great global flu epidemic of 1918, which hit the AEF at this time. In the first week of October alone doctors diagnosed over 15,000 cases among the troops, and there was some suspicion that Pershing himself had contracted the disease but had shaken it off.

Through it all, Pershing did all he could to keep the advance moving forward. Daily, he visited corps and division headquarters, listened to problems, judged commanders, and pushed to keep up the pressure on the Germans. At the end of each day, he returned to his train, where he reviewed reports and studied maps until the wee hours of the morning and then prepared to repeat the performance the next day. Those closest to him saw the strain he was under; his skin became pale, his hair was rapidly graying, and he appeared exhausted. To close confidants, Pershing admitted he felt as if he were carrying a tremendous burden. He was loathe to display emotion in front of any but a handful of close intimates. A glimpse of how Pershing thought about his public image can be found in the writings of Marshall, who, during the darkest hours of World War II, often reflected on the advice Pershing had given him: "a commander, no matter how weary, should never be seen burying his head on his desk, lest someone interpret it as a loss of hope. He must always give the impression of optimism."[11]

To this point, despite the difficulties and whatever his internal qualms, Pershing never evidenced any sign of despair or pessimism to those he commanded. Like his hero, Grant, he realized that battle was a contest of wills, and the man or side that made that last effort would be the winner. His First Army was bloodied, tattered, exhausted, but it was not just taking hits. On the contrary, it was hitting back and hitting hard. The Germans would eventually have thirty-six divisions on the American front, most of them first- or second-rate units. The Americans were losing men, but Army Chief of Staff March was pushing 300,000 men a month across the

Atlantic, and these replacements were steadily making their way to the front.

With no room to maneuver, Pershing knew he faced an appalling battle of attrition. As Lincoln once said of Grant, Pershing was a general who understood and could bear up to the terrible math of war. Americans were dying, but they were chewing up thirty-six enemy divisions that had no manpower reserves.

Under these conditions, victory would indeed come to the side that lasted the longest, and Pershing never doubted it would be the Americans. As he told one of his division commanders, Major General Henry Allen, "We are not getting on as we should, but by God! Allen, I was never so earnest in my life and we are going to get through.[12]

Marshall later said that watching Pershing's determination to keep driving ahead was the most memorable experience of the conflict, and Marshall wrote to him after the war:

> With distressingly heavy casualties, disorganized and only partially trained troops, supply problems of every character due to the devastated zone so rapidly crossed, inclement and cold weather, flu, stubborn resistance by the enemy on one of the strongest positions of the Western Front, pessimism on all sides and pleadings to halt the battle made by many of the influential members of the army, you persisted in your determination to force the fighting over all the difficulties and objections . . . nothing else in your leadership throughout was comparable to this.[13]

Taking stock of his commanders and the overall command arrangement, Pershing saw that big changes were required for both. With over a million men covering an eighty-three-mile front, the First Army had become too unwieldy for one man to control. To solve this problem, Pershing created the Second Army and placed

General Bullard in command, while simultaneously promoting General Liggett to command of the First Army. As he was making these command arrangements, Pershing also began the wholesale removal of generals who had not measured up to his exacting standards, and the promotion of those who did. Pershing demoted Cameron, then commanding the center corps, to command of a division, and the always aggressive Summerall received command of the V Corps. General Hines, a future chief of staff, had done well with his Fourth Division, so he took Bullard's II Corps, while General Joseph Dickman took Liggett's I Corps. Pershing also took the opportunity to move more of his veteran divisions, including General Menoher's magnificent Forty-Second Division, from St. Mihiel to the Argonne.

By October 14 the AEF was ready for another great push. Once more it came up short. His veteran divisions made progress, but only at appalling cost. Douglas MacArthur later related a visit his corps commander, Summerall, made during this phase of the fighting, as he was preparing to attack Cote de Chatillion:

> After offering General Summerall a cup of coffee he came alive. "Give me Chatillion, MacArthur or a list of five thousand casualties"
>
> Startled, MacArthur rose to the occasion and replied, "All right, General. We'll take it or my name will head the list."[14]

For five days the Americans pushed. But the Germans backed up only slightly, despite leaving a carpet of their own dead as they slowly retreated. By October 19 the First Army was once again a spent force. It had lost over 100,000 men and Liggett believed there were at least another 100,000 stragglers. Reluctantly, Pershing realized that his current methods were not working and ordered Liggett to halt operations for a short period of reorganization and retraining. While it looked bad on the American side, it was far worse for the Germans, who had to allow the Americans to decimate their best units in a forlorn hope of holding the line. When the American attack halted, Ludendorff said of the Argonne region, "Our best men lay on that bloody battlefield."[15]

In the meantime, the withdrawal of German divisions from the rest of the front, to be sent to the Meuse-Argonne region, made it possible for the French and British to realize some of their most spectacular gains of the war. By the end of October everyone knew the Germans were coming to the end of their tether. There were reports of German divisions mutinying and that tens of thousands of German soldiers were refusing to go back into the line. Pershing's intelligence section reported that in the previous four months the Germans had disbanded twenty-nine divisions and that fifty more had reduced the number of companies in their combat battalions. German replacements were arriving at the front without training and the walking wounded were being taken from hospital beds and fed back into the line. While Germany tottered, Turkey collapsed and surrendered on October 30. Austria-Hungary followed four days later. Germany was now alone.

<hr />

With peace in the air, Foch called a conference of Allied leaders to discuss the possibility and terms of an Armistice. The conference took place on October 25 and grew quite stormy. Haig pointed out that the Germans were retreating in good order and still launching punishing counterattacks when the Allies pushed too hard. He further pointed out that since the start of the new offensives the British and French armies had lost 250,000 men who had not been replaced. Continuing, he managed to anger Pershing by claiming that the Allies could not count on the American army as it was reorganizing after suffering due to its ignorance of modern warfare. Haig therefore advocated generous armistice terms, ones the Germans would find easy to accept.[16]

Pershing, along with Foch and Petain, disagreed with Haig's assessment of the war effort. All three commanders recognized that Germany was beaten, and the Allies were in a position to demand terms that would crush Germany's current military power. However, even Foch and Petain were ready to agree to terms that Pershing thought much too lenient. Pershing argued that the Allies should demand not an armistice, but Germany's unconditional surrender. Pershing was convinced that anything less than surrender would allow Germany to lick its wounds and rebuild it armies for another try at military victory. Over the course of several more meetings in late October and early November, Pershing made his opinion on a hard peace well known.

Thinking he had the president's permission to demand the Allies agree to his version of a negotiated peace, Pershing sent a detailed letter of his proposals to the Supreme War Council. The president, however, had already dispatched his most trusted advisor, Colonel House, to attend the next meeting of the council and Pershing should properly have sent his recommendations through House. House took this bypass as a deliberate slight. Pershing was now sick, probably fighting off the flu, and was unable to meet with House in person before the Supreme War Council met. At the council meeting, House was dismayed by Pershing's proposal to force an unconditional surrender. For House, this was a political matter, and Pershing was committing the worst of all sins: He was a general meddling in politics.[17] Pershing immediately realized he had blundered and beat a hasty retreat. He explained to House that his recital of unconditional surrender terms had been merely military advice, and he had not intended to intrude on political ground. But that did not end the matter.

When informed of Pershing's proposals to the Supreme War Council, Secretary Baker became upset enough to write his only letter of reprimand directed at Pershing. However, after hearing from House, Wilson determined that the whole incident had been a misunderstanding and had the letter quashed. Pershing had made a mistake, but it was a forgivable one. He was, after all, only interacting with the Allied political leadership just as he had been doing since his arrival in 1917 and as the president and secretary of war had expected him to do. Preoccupied by the day-to-day events at the front, Pershing had not noticed that the political ground beneath his feet had shifted and that the advent of peace had changed everything. Thoroughly chastened, Pershing beat a hasty retreat from peace proposals and other political matters and got back to winning the war.

By the end of October, Liggett had the First Army ready to make another effort. It was a completely retooled and remodeled army. Even veteran units were retrained in infantry tactics, particularly in the coordination and use of artillery to support an advance. Some infantry received special training in techniques for attacking strong points, while the rest were trained to bypass these defenses. Artillery batteries laid out supporting plans to use interdicting fires to isolate infantry objectives and conduct counterbattery fires against German artillery. Liggett instilled in his commanders the need to maximize supporting fires and the use of gas to suppress enemy defenses.[18]

While Liggett prepared his army, Pershing spent as much time as possible overseeing the building of roads, the laying of rail lines, and the stockpiling of thousands of tons of materiel for a new offensive. Extremely anxious that the attack succeed, he ordered his chief of staff and operations officer to drop all their other activities and focus entirely on transportation and communications problems. When he was not in Paris discussing armistice proposals, and as his other duties permitted, Pershing was out visiting his commanders. By now, they were all men whom Pershing trusted— smart, hard, and aggressive men who could be counted on to continue the attack until victory was achieved or their units had been bled white. Like Pershing, these were men capable of bearing up to the "terrible math" of modern war. This did not stop Pershing from issuing his corps commanders a hand-written letter telling each one that he would hold him personally responsible for the success or failure of his troops.[19]

On November 1, Pershing ordered his soldiers forward. A violent artillery barrage, which lit up the sky enough for front line soldiers to read newspapers in the dark, preceded the advance. Guns were firing so rapidly that they glowed red, and there was a real danger they would melt or warp. American artillery, supported by massed machine guns, crashed down on German positions, crossroads, ammo dumps, and other sensitive locations. At 5:30 A.M. the infantry went over the top. Pershing had begged for 500 tanks to join the assault, but only 18, all borrowed from the French, were available. Afterward he wrote that he considered it a matter of undying shame that the strongest industrial power in the world was never able to supply his army with a single tank.

From the start everything went right. This was a different American army than had fought in France before and was even qualitatively superior to what it had been just ten days before. The assault divisions were now all veteran units commanded by experienced and reliable commanders. They knew how to follow closely behind a rolling artillery barrage. They knew how to use airpower, which now flew in low to strafe enemy formations and support the infantrymen. In fact, the air arm had changed its priorities from contesting the air with German pilots to infantry support as a direct result of Pershing's policy to rotate pilots through the trenches to give them a taste of the misery that was part of the doughboys daily existence.

Pershing exalted, "For the first time the enemy's lines were completely broken through." The Germans were now facing a professional American army, which was methodically going about the business of grinding German divisions out of existence. In fact the First Army was moving so fast, it was running off Pershing's operational maps. Several times, Pershing had just finished dictating an order to capture a location, and even before the order could be typed up, received a call from Marshall that U.S. troops had over-run the place.

The German army was beaten. On the eleventh hour, of the eleventh day, of the eleventh month, the guns fell silent.

There was, however, one piece of irony. On November 5, Foch asked Pershing for six divisions for assignment to the French Tenth Army. It seemed that even in the final week of the war the amalgamation issue had not completely disappeared. Feeling expansive, Pershing consented to send the divisions, but insisted they form a separate American army. Again, there were protests, but Pershing stood firm, buoyed by a study done by his chief of staff that found: "Under American command identical divisions advanced farther against greater resistance in less time, and suffered less casualties."[20]

A few days after the war ended, Pershing ran into Clemenceau. "We fell into each others' arms, choked up and had to wipe away our tears. We had no differences to discuss that day." Harbord later commented, "The armistice thus ended two wars for us—the one with our friends, the other with our enemies."[21]

Liddell Hart, writing ten years after the war, said of Pershing, "It is sufficient to say that there was perhaps no other man who could have built the structure of the American army on the scale he planned. And without that army the war could hardly have been saved and could not have been won." After the war even Field Marshal Paul von Hindenburg admitted, "The American infantry in the Argonne won the war." Both statements are fair judgments.

CHAPTER 13

Chief of Staff

PERSHING'S RETURN TO THE UNITED STATES WAS CELE-brated with a tickertape parade down New York's Fifth Avenue. There was already talk of Pershing running for president and, while he did nothing to encourage this speculation, neither did he say or do anything to discourage it. Unlike General William Tecumseh Sherman, who famously said, "If nominated I will not run. If elected I will not serve," Pershing followed the advice of his father-in-law and kept silent on the matter. However, he did allow several of his Nebraska friends to form drafting committees to explore the matter without his official approval. When one of these committees placed his name on the Michigan ballot he finished a distant fifth.

After this setback, Pershing concluded that he had played the reluctant bride so effectively that the average American was convinced he did not want the job. So, during a reception in his honor at the Nebraska Society in April 1919, Pershing told the audience, "While I am in no sense seeking it, I feel that no patriotic American could decline to serve in that high position, if called to do so by the people." The next day the *Washington Post* headline read "PERSHING WILL RUN IF HE IS NOMINATED." This was not exactly true. Pershing was not willing to run for office, but he was willing to be asked. However, whatever hopes he might have harbored of becoming president were squashed by an early ballot in his home state where he won only his own county, and that by the slimmest of margins. It was obvious that the American people were not going to demand a Pershing presidency, and he quietly abandoned the idea.[1]

Several factors doomed the notion of a Pershing presidency. Among them were Pershing's failure to campaign openly and his espousal of unpopular causes, such as universal military training. Moreover, his campaign was poorly managed and run by amateurs. Without an effective machine at the state and local level, Pershing could not hope to corral the votes required to win in the primaries. Mostly, though, America was sick of war. Initial enthusiasm for the war had quickly worn off as the casualty list reached into the hundreds of thousands. While Americans were grateful for what Pershing had done to win, this did not translate into a desire to place one of the war's generals into the country's highest elected office.

As this political maneuvering was going on, Pershing went on a coast-to-coast tour of military bases, fulfilling the ceremonial role of an army commander without an army. It was a long year of train rides, inspection tours, and civic gatherings. Every town Pershing passed through wanted to throw a celebration with him as the guest of honor. During a side stop to tour the Culver City movie studios, he recognized a young flyer he had met in France, William Wellman, who was working as a twenty-three-year-old office boy at the studio. Pershing said hello and inquired if there were anything he could do for the young man. Wellman leaned in confidentially and said it would do him a great service if he would stop and talk to him for a few minutes in front of the executives before he left.

Later, Pershing broke away from the studio executives and led Wellman away for a private twenty-minute talk. The executives were much impressed and the next day Wellman was promoted to assistant director. He later became one of Hollywood's most respected and honored directors. He always claimed he owed his rise to Pershing taking the time to have a chat with him.

+———+

Pershing also used this time after the war to get reacquainted with his son Warren. As soon as the school semester ended, Pershing picked him up and took him on tour. Together they went tarpon fishing and on a quick trip to Europe. Pershing enjoyed his son's company and was sorry when it was time for him to return to school. Even though Warren boarded at Phillip Exeter Prep School, Pershing spent as much time as possible with him, insisting that his calendar be kept clear whenever Warren was on holiday. Warren later said that his father had only a modicum of success at supervising his education, although he received a constant stream of encouraging and admonishing letters from the "old gent" whenever his grades were slipping. One of Pershing's aides recalled that whenever Warren's grades would tumble, Pershing would complain that "he was disgracing the family," but then "he'd get a letter from Warren asking for ten dollars and he'd beam in delight over being needed in some way. He was always very proud of Warren and wanted to be close to him."[2]

Although Warren never went to West Point, he did enlist as a private during World War II after refusing his father's offer to get him assigned to George S. Patton's staff. He later went to Officer Candidate School and finished the war as a major in a combat engineer battalion on the Rhine River. Pershing had every reason to be proud of his son, who graduated from Yale with passable grades and was voted most likely to succeed. Additionally, he came out in the top five in three other voting categories—most handsome, most witty, most likeable. Warren also had the same fondness for the company of women as did his father, but settled down early on by marrying a beautiful and rich socialite, Muriel Bache Richards. Not that money played any part in his feelings for her, since Warren Pershing was already well on his way to earning his own millions on Wall Street. They had two sons, John and Richard, both of whom served in Vietnam, where Richard was killed in action in 1968 and was awarded the Silver Star for heroism. Their other son, John Pershing, retired from the Army in 1999 as a full colonel and later died from complications after surgery.

+>==<+

Eventually, Pershing's tours of inspection and thousands of social events came to an end. He returned to Washington to assume the duties of army chief of staff. It was not a good time to be chief. The Congress, in its typical shortsighted fashion, was set on economizing, and the military was its primary target. Throughout his term as chief of staff, Pershing was locked in a constant battle to maintain the army at a size he thought appropriate. Initially, Pershing persuaded Congress to agree to a standing army of 250,000 troops, deployed in nine divisions (three corps) across the country. These regular divisions would establish training camps where they would drill ROTC detachments and the local National Guard units to a level at least approximating the regulars.

Even this limited establishment was squashed a year later when Congress again cut the army budget and limited the size of the force to just over 100,000 soldiers. Pershing strongly opposed these cuts, which shrank the U.S. army to seventeenth in the world in size. However, even his considerable prestige could not overcome a political environment in which most believed that, if only the army were abolished and war production facilities dismantled, any future war would be avoided. The twin ideas of pacifism and isolationism, always present in the American body politic, were on the rise in the decades after World War I and it did not bode well for the army. In one later economizing measure, which was more a symbolic insult than a practical move, a motion was put before Congress to reduce Pershing's $18,000 pension. It took the personal intervention of the army chief of staff, Douglas MacArthur, to get the measure dropped.

Facing legislation he believed would destroy the army, Pershing set off on a continual round of speaking engagements. He now saw himself as morale-builder-in-chief and considered it his most pressing duty to visit as many posts as practical and talk to as many officers as possible to ensure the best of them stayed in the army despite low pay, slow advancement, and the conviction that the country did not need or care about them. At the same time, he took active measure to improve the army school system. This work is probably his most enduring legacy to the army.

He oversaw the revamping of the education officers received at their basic branch schools, the Command and General School, and the Army War College. Prior to his involvement, these schools had done a fair job at educating officers in handling their present circumstances, but did not teach them what would be required to lead massive armies in another major war. The value of this change in emphasis revealed itself in the early dark days of early World War II. By then, most of the officers who possessed professional experience in organizing, training, or leading large field formations during the Great War had passed from the scene, and a new crop of generals had arisen to lead the massive American armies in battle. That they were up to the task can be credited to Pershing, as all had learned how to handle their increased responsibilities in the army education system that Pershing had created.

Before he became president, Harry Truman had been the chairman of a Senate committee that oversaw military spending. He had grown used to seeing army officers appear before his committee and rather sheepishly request funding for one project or another. Late in World War II he once commented to another senator, "How did those cowed little men transform themselves into these giants that now bestride the globe?" In no small measure,

Pershing and the legacy he left to the army had created them in the years before the war. No matter how desperate the army budget situation became, Pershing never skimped on ensuring that the educational system was fully funded.

Pershing also remembered how the lack of an efficient general staff had seriously hindered America's mobilization for war in 1917. With President Warren Harding's support, Pershing created an efficient general staff system, the outline of which persists to this day. For the first time in its history the United States possessed a corps of officers whose main job was to plan for future operations and coordinate operations in the event of another conflict.

For almost two decades, the unheralded work of this small group of dedicated officers accomplished much of the planning that allowed the United States to mobilize so rapidly after Pearl Harbor. It had take eighteen months after America entered World War I before Pershing could launch his almost purely infantry armies into battle. By contrast, eighteen months after the Japanese attacked Pearl Harbor, the United States was already counterattacking in both the Pacific and European theaters. Moreover, the country was well on the way toward building armies, air forces, and fleets that would swamp America's enemies under a flood of materiel and munitions.

Pershing was not all-knowing, however. He most obviously failed when it came to appreciating the importance air power would have on future combat operations. Forgetting the air armadas with which Billy Mitchell had swept the skies over St. Mihiel and eventually over the Argonne-Meuse, Pershing often quipped that he could think of no battle in World War I in which air power made much of a difference. Although he was on hand to witness Mitchell's Chesapeake Bay demonstration in 1921, in which aircraft for the first time bombed and sank a battleship, Pershing still sided with the official navy report, which did not envision any future requirement for a large air force. Throughout his tenure as chief of staff, the Army Air Corps would remain at the bottom of the list when army budgets were submitted to Congress.

Pershing was also blind to the fact that the tank had redefined methods of war. He had seen the ponderous, unreliable monsters in combat and remained convinced that their best possible use was as infantry support. That they could suppress enemy pill-boxes and crush barbed wire was a proven fact. But to do those tasks, they only needed a speed of three miles an hour—as fast as a man could walk. The idea of concentrating fast-moving tanks in a massive armored punch that could crack the enemy line and then drive deep into his rear, leaving chaos in its wake, was a concept totally alien to everything Pershing knew about war.

It was not that Pershing was suddenly made dumb or short-sighted. He was, however, in this regard, as in many other things, a product of his times. He had learned the basics of his profession from men who had fought in the Civil War, and he himself had spent his early career chasing Indians or fighting technologically unsophisticated enemies, such as the Moros and Mexican bandits. And America's inability to produce large quantities of tanks and aircraft before World War I ended ensured that all his major battles were large-scale infantry attacks, supported by masses of artillery. In short, there was nothing in Pershing's training or professional experience that allowed him to grasp how new technology would radically change the face of war. Fortunately, however, Pershing kept men such as George S. Patton in the service, who had grown up in this time of technological ferment and who did possess the capacity to adapt to changing circumstances.

While he had actively sought the position of chief of staff, its attainment turned out to be rather anticlimactic for Pershing. The notion of overseeing the dismantling of the great military establishment he had commanded in war did not appeal to him, nor did many of the ceremonial duties the job required. He also found the constant requirement to negotiate with Congress tiresome. Though he stayed in the job until his retirement in 1924, he never really gave the impression that he worked very hard. In fact, he spent the last six months of his time as chief hiding in France, writing his memoirs, and visiting with Micheline Resco. He left the daily business of running the army and testifying in front of Congress to his deputy, General John L. Hines.

Pershing also found the Washington rumor mill infuriating, particularly as he was now a prime target. In one particularly galling episode, he was linked to a beautiful twenty-six-year-old, Louise Cromwell Brooks, who was also heiress to a $150 million fortune. Soon after she was seen in Pershing's company for dinner, she became romantically involved with one of his aides, Colonel John Quekemeyer, and had even promised to marry him just a week before she announced her engagement to Douglas MacArthur.

Two weeks after this marriage announcement, MacArthur received orders to report to the Philippines. The fact that he was at the top of the list for overseas duty meant nothing to the Washington gossips and word soon spread around town that MacArthur was being transferred in retaliation for Miss Brooks' spurning of Pershing. The situation was not helped by a comment Miss Brooks made to a reporter: "Jack wanted me to marry him. When I wouldn't, he wanted me to marry one of his colonels; I wouldn't do that—so here I am packing my trunks." Gossip got so bad that Pershing was finally forced to comment on the matter publicly: "It's all poppycock without the slightest foundation and based on the idlest gossip. If I were married to all of the ladies to whom the gossips have engaged me I would be a regular Brigham Young."[3]

Though Pershing respected MacArthur professionally and told many people that MacArthur was the best combat commander he had, he personally disliked him. Their relations were always cordial, but never intimate. He did not support MacArthur for the job of army chief of staff, preferring his own candidate, Fox Conner. But he did respect the job MacArthur did in that position. He particularly supported MacArthur's hard stand in the Congress against further cuts in the army budget. However, he found himself repelled by MacArthur's excessive ego and certain of his affectations, such as his corncob pipe. One Washington hostess remembered a postwar social event at which both men were present, with MacArthur monopolizing all conversation. When the evening was over and most of the guests had left, Pershing turned to her and asked, "Was there anybody else in the war?"[4]

+⧲⧲+

Pershing remained active in retirement, mostly through his appointment to head the American Battlefield Monument Commission, which conveniently allowed him to spend almost six months of the year in France with his beloved Micheline. The commission did not require much time, particularly as he was assisted by one of the ablest rising stars in the army, Major Dwight D. Eisenhower. In all probability it was Pershing who introduced the young Eisenhower to General Fox Conner, who later had Patton introduce him to Eisenhower. Conner became Eisenhower's mentor for almost the next twenty years and gave him the valuable advice to make friends with and stay close to George Marshall.

With time on his hands, Pershing turned to writing his memoirs. It was a task that would consume him for the next ten years of his life, and Pershing hated doing it. The final result, although it received the Pulitzer Prize, was a boring mish-mash that read more like an operations report than an account of his personal experience. This was due to Pershing's insistence that every person and unit be treated equally. When he completed the draft, he had several assistants go through it and tabulate how many times he mentioned each unit and major commander, and then recommend where he could insert additional material about those with fewer mentions. It produced a text that was dull in the extreme and in which the battle narratives were the dullest parts. George Marshall remarked, "the Meuse-Argonne account was too detailed for the general reader and not detailed enough for the military student. In endeavoring to mention each town and division commander, the battle has been made to appear a confused mass of little events, and from my point of view the big picture was lost."[5] In fact, the critical reception Pershing's book received and the effect it had on fellow officers was what convinced Marshall to never write his own memoirs, one of history's great losses.

Despite Pershing's attempts to speak well of everyone and avoid hurting anyone's feelings, inevitably a number of people were upset by what he had written. Those who served on the army staff in Washington were particularly miffed at what they perceived as insults to their ability and achievements. Secretary of War Baker explained to General March that, while Pershing could clearly see the troubles that beset himself, he had no appreciation for those of others. Pershing mentioned March only six times in the book and had intended to omit him altogether until warned by Marshall: "Everyone concerned with the war knows of your hostility to General March. But, to me, the fact remains that there was not another man, saving yourself, who could have filled the terribly difficult job of Chief of Staff in Washington. He did a remarkable job, in my opinion, which you should in no way belittle."[6] In the end, Pershing never said a negative word about March. Rather he damned him with faint praise.

March reacted explosively and considered the book a collection of lies. He quickly wrote his own book, called *The Nation at War,* where he gave vent to all of his emotions. In it he specifically said that Pershing was lacking in sufficient training to be a general, was afraid of big men, had created overlarge divisions, and was slow to commit his forces to combat. Further, he claimed that Pershing ordered cavalry be sent to France, even though there was obviously no need for it; and finally he claimed that Pershing made preposterous demands for huge amounts of materiel when the war was virtually over.

Pershing was furious at March's attacks and planned to respond in print. He was talked out of it by friends, including Harbord and Marshall. Later, Pershing worried that future historians would accept what he considered March's falsehoods as an honest account of events. He asked Harbord to begin collecting material that he could use to disprove March's assertions on a case-by-case basis. Harbord advised Pershing that doing so would just call attention to March's book and make matters worse. To pacify a still enraged Pershing, Harbord promised to write his own book to correct the historical record. When he heard about it, Secretary Baker implored Harbord to eschew personal attacks. He felt that both Pershing and March had performed superbly and that there was more then enough glory for both. Harbord took this advice and although he did not let all of March's attacks go unremarked, his book, *The American Army in France, 1917–1919,* is on the whole considerably more balanced and readable than either Pershing's or March's books.

Pershing stayed busy throughout the 1930s and was a leading advocate for military preparedness. He, like many farsighted observers, noted with alarm the rise of Adolf Hitler, and predicted another general European war, into which the Untied States would be drawn. Pershing also remained active in furthering the careers of officers he thought should have leading roles in any future major war. For instance, he strongly supported Marshall's promotion to brigadier general, over the objections of MacArthur, and when the chief of staff position opened up, he pushed for Marshall to be given the position, despite his having only one star. In a White House meeting with President Roosevelt, whom he later came to despise, Pershing said, "There is a young general over in the Army Plans Division who you need to have over here for a talk before you make your decision as to who will be the next chief of staff." This alone did not make Marshall the chief, but there is no doubt Pershing's influence helped.

In May 1941, his health failing, Pershing moved his residence to a suite at Walter Reed Army Hospital. There he passed the time reading, playing cards, and entertaining many of his friends from Nebraska and his war days. From time to time, he would even entertain some of the many strangers who just happened by and asked if the general was receiving visitors. He could, however, be picky about who he decided to meet. Once a middle-aged woman from Nebraska whose group had planted some trees in Pershing's honor wanted to visit and tell him about it.

"Is she good looking?" Pershing asked the nurse.

"Passable," the nurse replied.

"Tell her my doctor will not allow me to have visitors."

When war broke out in 1941 he found himself mostly neglected by those charged with commanding the great armies that fought it. No one asked for his advice, and what influence he had on the war rested on the memories of officers who had worked under him in the past. In persons like Patton and Marshall, this influence was considerable. In fact, before leaving for North Africa in 1942, Patton visited Pershing and asked for his blessing. Patton later commented on the meeting in his diary, saying that Pershing was hurt that no one was consulting him. But Patton also noted with sadness how little his former chief knew of modern war. Before he left the meeting, Pershing spoke about Patton's killing of two Mexicans with his pistol some years earlier. When Patton told him he was taking the same pistol to North Africa with him, Pershing replied, "I hope you get to kill some Germans with it."

Of course Pershing's influence could also be found in every officer educated for modern war in the military school system he had done so much to foster. He may not have personally grasped the intricacies of war in the modern age, but he ensured that those that came after him were ready to adapt what they had learned about the realities of brutal mechanized warfare. In a letter sent after VE Day, Eisenhower wrote to Pershing, "The stamp of Benning, Sill, Riley, and Leavenworth is on every battle in Europe and Africa. The sons of the men you led in battle in 1918 have much for which to thank you for."[7]

His influence was also felt in an unexpected corner. Word came to Pershing that when MacArthur and his senior commanders came ashore on the Philippine island of Jolo the first person to greet them was the old sultan of Jolo. He told MacArthur that he had submitted to Pershing as a young warrior in 1905 and had stayed loyal to the United States ever since. He also informed MacArthur that he and other Moros had proven their loyalty by killing any Japanese soldier who ventured away from his camp. While he may have felt neglected in Washington, Pershing was still remembered in the Moro heartland for his accomplishments, even four decades later.

+≡━≡+

On July 15, 1948, Pershing died peacefully in his sleep. Some 300,000 people lined the streets of Washington to watch his funeral possession. They were quiet and respectful, but for most, Pershing was a man from another era of whom they were only dimly aware. Behind his coffin marched sixteen active duty generals led by Dwight Eisenhower and Omar Bradley. As the procession inched forward there was a sudden downpour. Eisenhower asked Bradley if they should jump into one of the limousines provided for just this contingency. Bradley replied, "For Blackjack Pershing I think it would be proper if we walked in the rain."[8]

Long before his death, Pershing had made it known that he wanted to be buried among the men he had led in combat. He had selected a site in Arlington. His gravesite was adorned with the same simple stone that the government provides for any soldier and on it is just his name, state of birth, and rank: General of the Armies.

Pershing will probably never be ranked among the "great captains" of history. His men did not worship him as others had Caesar or Napoleon, and he never possessed the common touch that made masses of men love him and that inspired them to great feats. It never occurred to him that mass amateur armies, unlike the professionals with whom he had spent a career, required a bit of warmth to motivate them to accomplish great things. Furthermore, he never confronted an enemy he did not outnumber and outgun. Whether Pershing could have won great victories against insurmountable odds is one of those unknowable arguments of history.

At the same time, one cannot deny Pershing's accomplishments. Every major decision he made in peace and war was right. Some said this was due to the well known "Pershing luck," but even if fate did play a hand in events, it must be recognized that a good portion of his success rested on hard work and thorough preparation. When furnished with the required men, equipment, and supplies, Pershing always got the job done. In fact for every great victory won by a "great captain" against a superior foe, there is a general on the other side who failed despite having been given everything he required for success. If Pershing had one great virtue in the eyes of his superiors it was that given a mission and the tools to accomplish it, he would always succeed.

But the United State government did not give Pershing an army. They gave him two million armed, barely trained raw recruits, whose officers rarely knew any more about war then they did. It fell to Pershing to take this armed mob and turn them into soldiers and then turn those soldiers into an organized army capable of enduring and operating on the incredibly lethal modern battlefield. By any measure, this was a Herculean task and historians are in common agreement that there was no other soldier in the American army that could have done it.

A decade before, as he observed the Russo-Japanese War, Pershing had realized that the days of heroic leadership had ended. Inspiring commanders made good copy for the hometown press, but they no longer won wars. The great leaders of modern mass warfare would be the soldiers who could master the intricacies of logistics and management. There would never again be an opportunity to win a campaign or a war with one bold stroke or a perfectly executed slashing cavalry charge. What mattered in 1918 was who could amass the most men and firepower at a specific point of battle, and then sustain that fight for weeks or months. At this Pershing proved to be a true master.

If the mark of true genius is to be able to adapt to changing circumstance, then Pershing was a military genius. His entire career had been spent leading small units in small operations against insurgents. It was not until 1916 that he was given command of a force greater then ten thousand men, and even that was widely disbursed on the equivalent of guerrilla operations. In under two years Pershing had to discard almost everything he had learned about practical soldiering and train himself to be a manager of massive armies, fighting as part of an unwieldy coalition, on a battlefield of previously unimaginable lethality and horror. Pershing accomplished this self-imposed task and then created an army in his likeness that went on to ultimate victory just months after it was committed to combat on a massive scale.

All of what history calls the "great captains" were eventually defeated or fought in a doomed cause. Perhaps because he never lost a battle, or maybe just because of the American tendency not to over-glorify its leaders, history does not usually place Pershing in the ranks of the great captains. But if the qualifications for joining this elite group were solely based on military achievement on the battlefield, Pershing would surely qualify. And if the title of great captain does continue to elude him, then he will always be able to hold to a judgment he would have considered more dear—he was a great soldier.

Notes

Chapter 1

1. Unpublished Pershing memoir, National Archives. Unless otherwise noted, all quotes in this book up until World War I come from these memoirs.
2. Donald Smythe, *Guerrilla Warrior: The Early Life of John J. Pershing* (New York: Charles Scribner's Sons, 1973), p. 9.
3. Smythe, p. 11.
4. Collected from various pages of Smythe's *Guerrilla Warrior.*
5. Smythe, p. 15.
6. Smythe, p. 33.
7. Smythe, p. 33
8. Smythe, p. 45.

Chapter 2

1. The rest of Wheeler's command consisted of Pershing's old regiment, the Sixth Cavalry, and the all-volunteer Rough Riders.
2. Jacob Astor later became the richest man to lose his life on the *Titanic.*
3. As quoted in Smythe, p. 52.
4. Donald Smythe, "Pershing in the Spanish American War," *Military Affairs,* Vol. 30, No.1 (Spring, 1966), p. 29.
5. Ibid., p. 30.

Chapter 3

1. Richard Goldhurst, *Pipe Clay and Drill* (New York: Readers Digest Press, 1977), p. 105.
2. As quoted in Smythe, p. 84.
3. Smythe, p. 90.
4. Smythe, p. 103.

Chapter 4

1. Smythe, p. 113.
2. Smythe, p. 116.
3. *The Romance of Frances Warren Pershing* (author unknown). This multipart article can be found at http://www.umcwy.org/Pershings /02%20Pershing%20Romance.htm.
4. Smythe, p. 121.
5. Smythe, p. 126.
6. Smith, p. 97.
7. Smythe, p. 135.
8. Smythe, p. 138.

Chapter 5

1. Smythe, p. 147.
2. Smythe, p. 198.
3. Smythe, p. 214.
4. Smythe, p. 215.
5. Smythe, p. 217.

Chapter 6

1. Richard O'Connor, *Black Jack Pershing* (New York: Doubleday & Company, 1961), p. 122.
2. O'Connor, p. 136.

Chapter 7

1. Hew Strachan, *The First World War* (London: Penguin Group, 2003), p. 184.
2. Martin Evans, *Battles of World War I* (London: Arcturus Publishing, 2004).
3. Strachan, p. 242.

4. Donald Smythe, *Pershing: General of the Armies* (Bloomington: Indiana University Press, 1986), p. 8.
5. Frank E. Vandiver, *Black Jack: The Life and Times of John J. Pershing*, vol. 2 (College Station and London: Texas A & M University Press, 1977), p. 676.
6. John Pershing, *My Experiences in the World War: Volume II* (New York: Frederick A. Stokes Company, 1931), p. 3.
7. Pershing, p. 17.
8. Smythe, p. 4.
9. Smythe, p. 6.
10. Smythe, p. 16.
11. Pershing, p. 18.
12. Richard Goldhurst, *Pipe Clay and Drill* (New York: Readers Digest Press, 1977), p. 259.
13. From a speech given by Frank Vandiver to the U.S. Air Force Academy in 1963, found at: http://www.worldwa-r1.com/dbc/pervandiver.htm.
14. Goldhurst, p. 232.
15. Vandiver, 1963, found at: http://www.worldwar1.com/dbc/pervandiver.htm.
16. Ibid.
17. Vandiver, p. 689.
18. Pershing, p. 23.
19. Pershing, p. 32.
20. Goldhurst, p. 259.
21. Goldhurst, p. 360.
22. Michael McCarthy, *"Lafayette, We Are Here": The War College Division and American Military Planning for the AEF in World War I*, found at http://www.worldwar1.com/dbc/plan2.htm.

Chapter 8

1. Smythe, p. 19.
2. Pershing, p. 59.
3. Smythe, p. 21.
4. Pershing, p. 63.
5. Smythe, p. 22.
6. Smythe, p. 25.
7. John Eisenhower, *Yanks: The Epic Story of the American Army in World War I* (New York: Simon & Schuster, 2001), p. 47.
8. Edward M. Coffman, "Peyton C. March: Greatest Unsung American General of World War I," *The Quarterly Journal of Military History* (Summer 2006).

9. Ibid.

Chapter 9

1. Mark E. Grotelueschen, *The AEF Way of War: The American Army and Combat in World War I* (London: Cambridge University Press, 2006).
2. Mark E. Grotelueschen, *Doctrine Under Fire: American Artillery Employment in World War I* (Westport, CT: Greenwood Press, 2001).
3. David G. Fivecoat, *Fine Conduct Under Fire: The Tactical Effectiveness of the 165th Infantry Regiment in the First World War,* unpublished thesis, U.S. Army Command and General Staff College, 1993.
4. Vandiver, p. 798.
5. Smythe, p. 55.
6. Vandiver, p. 778.
7. Smythe, p. 58.
8. Smythe, p. 163.
9. Smythe, p. 166.
10. Smythe, p. 166.
11. As quoted in Vandiver, p. 782.
12. As quoted in Vandiver, p. 783.
13. All of the following information on Ms. Resco is extracted from Smythe, pp. 296–301.
14. Smythe, p. 322.
15. Richard Stewart, *American Military History: Volume II* (Washington: Center of Military History, United States Army, 2005), p. 25.
16. Stewart, p. 26.
17. Smythe, p. 69.
18. Smythe, p. 68.
19. Smythe, p. 68.

Chapter 10

1. Stewart, p. 27.
2. Smythe, p. 69.
3. Smythe, p. 70.
4. Smythe, p. 77.
5. Pershing, p. 305.
6. Pershing, p. 307.
7. Smythe, p. 97.
8. Pershing, p. 28.

9. Pershing, p. 29.
10. Vandiver, p. 887.
11. Eisenhower, p. 114.
12. Eisenhower, p. 130.
13. Eisenhower, p. 132.
14. Smythe, p. 129.
15. Smythe. p. 131.
16. Smythe, p. 138.
17. Vandiver, p. 898.
18. Smythe, p. 141.
19. Great War Society Files, found at http://www.worldwar1.com/dbc /2marne.htm.
20. James Lacey, *Takedown: The 3rd Infantry Division's Twenty-one Day Assault on Baghdad* (Annapolis: United States Naval Press, 2007).
21. Stewart, p. 34.
22. Stewart, p. 38.
23. Smythe, p. 157.
24. Stewart, p. 38.
25. Pershing, Vol II, p. 161.
26. Strachan, p. 298.
27. Pershing, Vol II, p. 162.
28. Strachan, p. 311.

Chapter 11

1. This encounter is drawn from Smythe Vol. II, pages 174–177 and Pershing, pp. 243–250.
2. Pershing, p. 254.
3. Pershing, p. 255.
4. Pershing, p. 260.
5. As quoted in Smythe, Vol II, p. 185.
6. Pershing, p. 267.

Chapter 12

1. Alan Axelrod, *Patton: A Biography* (New York: Palgrave MacMillan, 2006), p. 148.
2. By the end of the second week of the offensive the First Army could only muster seventeen operating tanks.
3. James Cooke, *Pershing and His Generals: Command and Staff in the AEF* (Westport, CT: Praeger, 1997), p. 126.
4. Cooke, p. 127.
5. Smythe, p. 191.

6. Pershing, p. 283.
7. As quoted in Smythe, p. 196.
8. Smythe, p. 200.
9. As quoted in Smythe, p. 200.
10. As quoted in Smythe, p. 205.
11. Smythe, p. 209.
12. Smythe, p. 209.
13. As quoted in Smythe, p. 208.
14. Eisenhower, p. 256.
15. Smythe, p. 219.
16. Smythe, p. 220.
17. Vandiver, p. 983
18. Stewart, p. 40.
19. Smythe, p. 223.
20. Smythe, p. 227.
21. Smythe, p. 233.

Chapter 13

1. Smythe, p. 272.
2. O'Conner, p. 369.
3. Goldhurst, p. 322.
4. Smythe, p. 278.
5. Smythe, p. 392.
6. Smythe, p. 293.
7. Smythe, p. 306.
8. Smythe, p. 309.

Index

generals, 111–12, 126, 131, 152, 162–3, 184

George, David Lloyd, 87, 100, 131–2

Germany, ix, 1, 3–4, 59, 85–7, 92–3, 96, 99, 103, 110–11, 114, 127–30, 133–4, 136–49, 151, 155–6, 158, 161–6, 169–77 See Hutier tactics; Erich Ludendorff; World War I

Ghost Dance uprising, 15–17, 73

Goethals, George, 105, 119

Grant, Ulysses S., x, 11, 32, 91, 94, 106, 158, 163, 170–1

Great Britain, viii, ix, 2, 86–8, 92–3, 95–6, 99–100, 102–3, 109, 111, 113, 115–17, 121–3, 129–36, 139–40, 147–8, 151, 153–4, 157, 166–8, 173 See amalgamation; David Lloyd George; World War I

Haig, Douglas, 87, 110, 116–17, 129, 131, 133–5, 139, 173–4

Halleck, Henry, 106

Harbord, James, G. 32, 94, 97, 101–2, 106, 120, 140–1, 146–7, 169, 177, 189

Harding, Warren, 184

Hart, Basil Liddell, 112, 177

Hines, John L., 165, 172, 186

Hitler, Adolph, 85–6, 189

Hodges, Courtney, 80

House, Edward, 119, 131, 174

Huerta, Victoriano, 78–9

Hutier tactics, ix, 133

Indian Wars, viii, 13–17, 33–4, 185 See Apache Wars; Wounded Knee

industrialization, 109–12 See modern warfare

infantry divisions See First; Forty-Second; Fourth; Second; Third

Iraq War, viii, 35, 62, 144

Japan, 51–4, 57, 93

juramentados (oath-takers), 35–6, 65–7

Kernan, Francis, 118–20

King George V, 95

Lake Lanao, 46, 61, 63

Liggett, Hunter, 113, 145, 163–5, 169, 171–2, 175

Lincoln, Abraham, 162, 171

logistics, 4, 32, 54, 99–100, 102–3, 105–6, 117–21, 130, 132–4, 136, 141, 148–9, 151, 169–71, 175, 193

Ludendorff, Erich, 137, 142, 145, 147, 149, 151, 173

MacArthur, Douglas, vii, ix, x, 135, 172, 186, 189, 191

malaria, 26, 31

March, Peyton, 27, 104–6, 119, 170–1, 188–9

Marshall, George C., vii, ix, x, 91–2, 104, 115–16, 136, 138, 140, 155, 160, 170–1, 176–7, 187–90

McClellan, George, 162

McKinley, William, 25, 49

McNair, Lesley, 80

Meuse-Argonne offensive, x, 1, 3–4, 154, 158–77, 184, 188

Mexican Expedition, 79–82, 88, 185

Mexican-American War, viii, 32

Petain, Marshall Philippe, 2, 87–8,
101, 103, 116, 131, 133,
135, 139–40, 149, 154, 174
Philippine-American War, viii,
33–47, 49, 55
Philippines, viii, 33–47, 49, 55,
57–73, 127, 186, 191 *See*
Bud Bagsak; Camp Vickers;
Filipinos; Fort McKinley;
juramentados; Moros;
Philippine-American War
public opinion, 77–9, 85

quartermaster corps, 22, 24–5,
31–2, 82–3, 105, 117

racism, 20, 24
Resco, Micheline, 124–5, 186–7
Roosevelt, Theodore, 20–1, 23,
31, 49–50, 52, 54–5, 60, 73,
89–90, 92, 94–5
Rough Riders, 20–1, 29–30, 55,
95
Russia, 51–4, 59, 110, 129, 147,
193
Russo-Japanese War, 51–4, 193

St. Mihiel, 3, 149, 152, 154–6,
159–60, 162, 184
San Juan Hill, 25–31, 49, 55, 62
Second Battle of the Marne,
143–4
Second Infantry Division (U.S.),
126, 140–1, 145–7, 160
September 11, 2001, 66
Shaw, George, 70–1
Sherman, William Tecumseh, 179
Sibert, William L., 104, 115–16,
126–7
Soissons, 145
Somme, 87, 110
Spaatz, Carl, 80

Spanish-American War, viii,
23–33, 49, 55, 80, 88–90 *See*
San Juan Hill
Summerall, Charles, 137, 146, 172
Sumner, Samuel, 40, 43
Supreme War Council, 131–2,
134, 174

Taft, William Howard, 52, 58–60
Tenth Cavalry Regiment ("Buffalo
Soldiers") (United States), 20,
22, 24–7, 31, 55
terrorists, *See juramentados*
III Corps (Third Corps) (U.S.),
164–5
Third Infantry Division (U.S.),
140, 143–5, 169
training, *See* military training
trench warfare, ix-x, 112–13, 126,
161, 163
Truman, Harry, 183

U.S. Army, vii-viii, x, 1–5, 13,
35–6, 90, 92–8, 101–4, 106,
112–16, 119–21, 125–8,
135–49, 154–70, 177,
182–7, 190–3 aggressiveness
of, x, 144, 146–7, 154–5,
163, 169 Air Corps, 93,
184–5 creation of, vii-x, 5,
92–5, 97–8, 103, 116,
148–9, 156, 177, 192–3 *See*
First United States Army
funding, 182–7 the "lost
battalion," 161 school
system, x, 183–4, 190–1
Services of Supply (SOS),
120–1 *See* amalgamation;
American Expeditionary
Force (AEF); corps; First U.S.
Army; generals; infantry
divisions; Iraq War; modern